United States Government Accountability Office

By the Comptroller General of the
United States

July 2018

GOVERNMENT AUDITING STANDARDS

2018 Revision

GAO-18-568G

United States Government Accountability Office

By the Comptroller General of the United States

July 2018

GOVERNMENT AUDITING STANDARDS

2018 Revision

The 2018 revision of *Government Auditing Standards* is effective for financial audits, attestation engagements, and reviews of financial statements for periods ending on or after June 30, 2020, and for performance audits beginning on or after July 1, 2019. Early implementation is not permitted. The 2018 revision of *Government Auditing Standards* supersedes the 2011 revision (GAO-12-331G, December 2011), the 2005 *Government Auditing Standards: Guidance on GAGAS Requirements for Continuing Professional Education* (GAO-05-568G, April 2005), and the 2014 *Government Auditing Standards: Guidance for Understanding the New Peer Review Ratings* (D06602, January 2014). The 2018 revision should be used until further updates and revisions are made. An electronic version of this document can be accessed on GAO's Yellow Book web page at http://www.gao.gov/yellowbook.

GAO-18-568G

Contents

Letter	1

Chapter 1: Foundation and Principles for the Use and Application of Government Auditing Standards	3
Introduction	3
Types of GAGAS Users	6
Types of GAGAS Engagements	7
Financial Audits	7
Attestation Engagements and Reviews of Financial Statements	9
Performance Audits	10
Terms Used in GAGAS	15
The GAGAS Format	16

Chapter 2: General Requirements for Complying with Government Auditing Standards	18
Complying with GAGAS	18
Relationship between GAGAS and Other Professional Standards	20
Stating Compliance with GAGAS in the Audit Report	22

Chapter 3: Ethics, Independence, and Professional Judgment	25
Ethical Principles	25
The Public Interest	26
Integrity	26
Objectivity	27
Proper Use of Government Information, Resources, and Positions	27
Professional Behavior	28
Independence	28
GAGAS Conceptual Framework Approach to Independence	31
Provision of Nonaudit Services to Audited Entities	43
Consideration of Specific Nonaudit Services	50
Documentation	57
Professional Judgment	58

Chapter 4: Competence and Continuing Professional Education	63
Competence	63
Continuing Professional Education	67

Chapter 5: Quality Control and Peer Review	81
Quality Control and Assurance	81
System of Quality Control	81
Leadership Responsibilities for Quality within the Audit Organization	82
Independence, Legal, and Ethical Requirements	82
Initiation, Acceptance, and Continuance of Engagements	84
Human Resources	84
Engagement Performance	86
Monitoring of Quality	91
External Peer Review	96
Additional Requirements for Audit Organizations Not Affiliated with Recognized Organizations	102

Chapter 6: Standards for Financial Audits	109
Additional GAGAS Requirements for Conducting Financial Audits	109
Compliance with Standards	109
Licensing and Certification	110
Auditor Communication	110
Results of Previous Engagements	111
Investigations or Legal Proceedings	112
Noncompliance with Provisions of Laws, Regulations, Contracts, and Grant Agreements	112
Findings	113
Audit Documentation	116
Availability of Individuals and Documentation	117
Additional GAGAS Requirements for Reporting on Financial Audits	118
Reporting the Auditors' Compliance with GAGAS	118
Reporting on Internal Control; Compliance with Provisions of Laws, Regulations, Contracts, and Grant Agreements; and Instances of Fraud	119
Presenting Findings in the Audit Report	121
Reporting Findings Directly to Parties outside the Audited Entity	122
Obtaining and Reporting the Views of Responsible Officials	123
Reporting Confidential or Sensitive Information	125
Distributing Reports	126

Chapter 7: Standards for Attestation Engagements and Reviews of Financial Statements		127
	Examination Engagements	128
	Compliance with Standards	128
	Licensing and Certification	129
	Auditor Communication	129
	Results of Previous Engagements	130
	Investigations or Legal Proceedings	130
	Noncompliance with Provisions of Laws, Regulations, Contracts, and Grant Agreements	131
	Findings	132
	Examination Engagement Documentation	135
	Availability of Individuals and Documentation	136
	Reporting the Auditors' Compliance with GAGAS	136
	Reporting Deficiencies in Internal Control	137
	Reporting on Noncompliance with Provisions of Laws, Regulations, Contracts, and Grant Agreements or Instances of Fraud	138
	Presenting Findings in the Report	139
	Reporting Findings Directly to Parties outside the Audited Entity	139
	Obtaining and Reporting the Views of Responsible Officials	140
	Reporting Confidential or Sensitive Information	142
	Distributing Reports	143
	Review Engagements	144
	Compliance with Standards	144
	Licensing and Certification	144
	Noncompliance with Provisions of Laws, Regulations, Contracts, and Grant Agreements	145
	Reporting Auditors' Compliance with GAGAS	145
	Distributing Reports	146
	Agreed-Upon Procedures Engagements	147
	Compliance with Standards	147
	Licensing and Certification	147
	Noncompliance with Provisions of Laws, Regulations, Contracts, and Grant Agreements	148
	Reporting Auditors' Compliance with GAGAS	148
	Distributing Reports	149
	Reviews of Financial Statements	150
	Compliance with Standards	150
	Licensing and Certification	150
	Noncompliance with Provisions of Laws, Regulations, Contracts, and Grant Agreements	151

Reporting Auditors' Compliance with GAGAS	151
Distributing Reports	152

Chapter 8: Fieldwork Standards for Performance Audits — 154

Planning	154
Auditor Communication	158
Investigations or Legal Proceedings	159
Results of Previous Engagements	160
Assigning Auditors	160
Preparing a Written Audit Plan	161
Conducting the Engagement	162
Nature and Profile of the Program and User Needs	162
Determining Significance and Obtaining an Understanding of Internal Control	165
Assessing Internal Control	168
Internal Control Deficiencies Considerations	169
Information Systems Controls Considerations	171
Provisions of Laws, Regulations, Contracts, and Grant Agreements	174
Fraud	175
Identifying Sources of Evidence and the Amount and Type of Evidence Required	177
Using the Work of Others	177
Supervision	179
Evidence	179
Overall Assessment of Evidence	185
Findings	186
Audit Documentation	190
Availability of Individuals and Documentation	192

Chapter 9: Reporting Standards for Performance Audits — 194

Reporting Auditors' Compliance with GAGAS	194
Report Format	195
Report Content	195
Reporting Findings, Conclusions, and Recommendations	199
Reporting on Internal Control	201
Reporting on Noncompliance with Provisions of Laws, Regulations, Contracts, and Grant Agreements	203
Reporting on Instances of Fraud	204
Reporting Findings Directly to Parties outside the Audited Entity	204

	Obtaining the Views of Responsible Officials	206
	Report Distribution	207
	Reporting Confidential or Sensitive Information	208
	Discovery of Insufficient Evidence after Report Release	210

Glossary	211

Acknowledgments		222
	Comptroller General's Advisory Council on Government Auditing Standards (2016-2020)	222
	GAO Project Team	223
	Staff Acknowledgments	223

Figures		
	Figure 1: Generally Accepted Government Auditing Standards Conceptual Framework for Independence	61
	Figure 2: Independence Considerations for Preparing Accounting Records and Financial Statements	62
	Figure 3: Developing Peer Review Communications for Observed Matters in Accordance with Generally Accepted Government Auditing Standards	108
	Figure 4: Consideration of Internal Control in a Generally Accepted Government Auditing Standards Performance Audit	193

Abbreviations

AICPA	American Institute of Certified Public Accountants
AR-C	AICPA *Codification of Statements on Standards for Accounting and Review Services*
AT-C	AICPA *Codification of Statements on Standards for Attestation Engagements*
AU-C	AICPA *Codification of Statements on Auditing Standards*
CPA	certified public accountant
CPE	continuing professional education
GAGAS	generally accepted government auditing standards
IAASB	International Auditing and Assurance Standards Board
IT	information technology
OMB	Office of Management and Budget
PCAOB	Public Company Accounting Oversight Board
SAS	Statements on Auditing Standards
SSAE	Statements on Standards for Attestation Engagements

This is a work of the U.S. government and is not subject to copyright protection in the United States. The published product may be reproduced and distributed in its entirety without further permission from GAO. However, because this work may contain copyrighted images or other material, permission from the copyright holder may be necessary if you wish to reproduce this material separately.

GAO
U.S. GOVERNMENT ACCOUNTABILITY OFFICE

441 G St. N.W.
Washington, DC 20548

**Comptroller General
of the United States**

Audits provide essential accountability and transparency over government programs. Given the current challenges facing governments and their programs, the oversight provided through auditing is more critical than ever. Government auditing provides the objective analysis and information needed to make the decisions necessary to help create a better future. The professional standards presented in this 2018 revision of *Government Auditing Standards* (known as the Yellow Book) provide a framework for performing high-quality audit work with competence, integrity, objectivity, and independence to provide accountability and to help improve government operations and services. These standards, commonly referred to as generally accepted government auditing standards (GAGAS), provide the foundation for government auditors to lead by example in the areas of independence, transparency, accountability, and quality through the audit process.

This revision contains major changes from, and supersedes, the 2011 revision. These changes, summarized below, reinforce the principles of transparency and accountability and strengthen the framework for high-quality government audits.

- All chapters are presented in a revised format that differentiates requirements and application guidance related to those requirements.

- Supplemental guidance from the appendix of the 2011 revision is either removed or incorporated into the individual chapters.

- The independence standard is expanded to state that preparing financial statements from a client-provided trial balance or underlying accounting records generally creates significant threats to auditors' independence, and auditors should document the threats and safeguards applied to eliminate and reduce threats to an acceptable level or decline to perform the service.

- The peer review standard is modified to require that audit organizations comply with their respective affiliated organization's peer review requirements and GAGAS peer review requirements. Additional requirements are provided for audit organizations not affiliated with recognized organizations.

- The standards include a definition for waste.

- The performance audit standards are updated with specific considerations for when internal control is significant to the audit objectives.

Effective with the implementation dates for the 2018 revision of *Government Auditing Standards*, GAO is also retiring *Government Auditing Standards: Guidance on GAGAS Requirements for Continuing Professional Education* (GAO-05-568G, April 2005) and *Government Auditing Standards: Guidance for Understanding the New Peer Review Ratings* (D06602, January 2014).

This revision of the standards has gone through an extensive deliberative process, including public comments and input from the Comptroller General's Advisory Council on Government Auditing Standards (Advisory Council). The Advisory Council consists of experts in financial and performance auditing and reporting from federal, state, and local government; the private sector; and academia. The views of all parties were thoroughly considered in finalizing the standards.

The 2018 revision of *Government Auditing Standards* is effective for financial audits, attestation engagements, and reviews of financial statements for periods ending on or after June 30, 2020, and for performance audits beginning on or after July 1, 2019. Early implementation is not permitted.

An electronic version of this document can be accessed at http://www.gao.gov/yellowbook.

I extend special thanks to the members of the Advisory Council for their extensive input and feedback throughout the process of developing and finalizing the standards.

Gene L. Dodaro
Comptroller General of the United States

July 2018

Chapter 1: Foundation and Principles for the Use and Application of Government Auditing Standards

1.01 This chapter provides guidance for engagements conducted in accordance with generally accepted government auditing standards (GAGAS). This chapter also

a. explains the types of auditors and audit organizations that may employ GAGAS to conduct their work,

b. identifies the types of engagements that may be conducted in accordance with GAGAS, and

c. explains terminology that is commonly used in GAGAS.

Introduction

1.02 The concept of accountability for use of public resources and government authority is key to our nation's governing processes. Management and officials entrusted with public resources are responsible for carrying out public functions and providing service to the public effectively, efficiently, economically, and ethically within the context of the statutory boundaries of the specific government program.

1.03 As reflected in applicable laws, regulations, agreements, and standards, management and officials of government programs are responsible for providing reliable, useful, and timely information for transparency and accountability of these programs and their operations. Legislators, oversight bodies, those charged with governance, and the public need to know whether (1) management and officials manage government resources and use their authority properly and in compliance with laws and regulations; (2) government programs are achieving their objectives and desired outcomes; and (3) government services are provided effectively, efficiently, economically, and ethically.

1.04 "Those charged with governance" refers to the individuals responsible for overseeing the strategic direction of the entity and obligations related to the accountability of the entity. This includes overseeing the financial reporting process, subject matter, or program under audit, including related internal controls. Those charged with governance may also be part of the entity's management. In some audited entities, multiple parties may be charged with governance, including oversight bodies, members or staff of legislative committees, boards of directors, audit committees, or parties contracting for the engagement.

Chapter 1: Foundation and Principles for the Use and Application of Government Auditing Standards

1.05 Government auditing is essential in providing accountability to legislators, oversight bodies, those charged with governance, and the public. GAGAS engagements provide an independent, objective, nonpartisan assessment of the stewardship, performance, or cost of government policies, programs, or operations, depending upon the type and scope of the engagement.

1.06 The professional standards and guidance contained in this document provide a framework for conducting high-quality engagements with competence, integrity, objectivity, and independence. Auditors of government entities, entities that receive government awards, and other entities, as required by law or regulation or as they elect, may use these standards. Overall, GAGAS contains standards for engagements comprising individual requirements that are identified by terminology as discussed in paragraphs 2.02 through 2.10. GAGAS contains requirements and guidance dealing with ethics, independence, auditors' professional judgment and competence, quality control, peer review, conducting the engagement, and reporting.

1.07 Engagements conducted in accordance with GAGAS provide information used for oversight, accountability, transparency, and improvements of government programs and operations. GAGAS contains requirements and guidance to assist auditors in objectively obtaining and evaluating sufficient, appropriate evidence and reporting the results. When auditors conduct their work in this manner and comply with GAGAS in reporting the results, their work can lead to improved government management, better decision making and oversight, effective and efficient operations, and accountability and transparency for resources and results.

1.08 Laws, regulations, contracts, grant agreements, and policies frequently require that engagements be conducted in accordance with GAGAS. In addition, many auditors and audit organizations voluntarily choose to conduct their work in accordance with GAGAS. The requirements and guidance in GAGAS in totality apply to engagements pertaining to government entities, programs, activities, and functions, and to government assistance administered by contractors, nonprofit entities, and other nongovernmental entities when the use of GAGAS is required or voluntarily adopted.

1.09 The following are some of the laws, regulations, and other authoritative sources that require the use of GAGAS:

a. The Inspector General Act of 1978, as amended (5 U.S.C. App.), requires that the federal inspectors general appointed under that act comply with GAGAS for audits of federal establishments, organizations, programs, activities, and functions. The act further states that the inspectors general shall take appropriate steps to assure that any work performed by nonfederal auditors complies with GAGAS.

b. The Chief Financial Officers Act of 1990 (Public Law 101-576), as expanded by the Government Management Reform Act of 1994 (Public Law 103-356), requires that GAGAS be followed in audits of major executive branch departments' and agencies' financial statements. The Accountability of Tax Dollars Act of 2002 (Public Law 107-289) generally extends this requirement to most executive agencies not subject to the Chief Financial Officers Act.

c. The Single Audit Act Amendments of 1996 (Public Law 104-156) requires that GAGAS be followed in audits of state and local governments and nonprofit entities that receive federal awards. Subpart F of OMB's *Uniform Administrative Requirements, Cost Principles, and Audit Requirements for Federal Awards* (2 C.F.R. part 200), which provides the government-wide guidelines and policies on conducting audits to comply with the Single Audit Act, reiterates the requirement to use GAGAS.

1.10 Other laws, regulations, or authoritative sources may require the use of GAGAS. For example, auditors at the state and local government levels may be required by state and local laws and regulations to follow GAGAS. Also, auditors may be required by the terms of an agreement or contract to follow GAGAS. Auditors may also be required to follow GAGAS by federal audit guidelines pertaining to program requirements. Being aware of such other laws, regulations, or authoritative sources may assist auditors in performing their work in accordance with the required standards.

1.11 Even if not required to do so, auditors may find it useful to follow GAGAS in conducting engagements pertaining to federal, state, and local government programs as well as engagements pertaining to state and local government awards that contractors, nonprofit entities, and other nongovernmental entities administer. Though not formally required to do so, many audit organizations, both in the United States and in other countries, voluntarily follow GAGAS.

Chapter 1: Foundation and Principles for the
Use and Application of Government Auditing
Standards

Types of GAGAS Users

1.12 GAGAS provides standards that are used by a wide range of auditors and audit organizations that audit government entities, entities that receive government awards, and other entities. These auditors and audit organizations may also be subject to additional requirements unique to their environments. Examples of the various types of users who may be required or may elect to use GAGAS include the following:

a. Contract auditors: audit organizations that specialize in conducting engagements pertaining to government acquisitions and contract administration

b. Certified public accounting firms: public accounting organizations in the private sector that provide audit, attestation, or review services under contract to government entities or recipients of government funds

c. Federal inspectors general: government audit organizations within federal agencies that conduct engagements and investigations relating to the programs and operations of their agencies and issue reports both to agency management and to third parties external to the audited entity

d. Federal agency internal auditors: internal government audit organizations associated with federal agencies that conduct engagements and investigations relating to the programs and operations of their agencies

e. Municipal auditors: elected or appointed officials in government audit organizations in the United States at the city, county, and other local government levels

f. State auditors: elected or appointed officials in audit organizations in the governments of the 50 states, the District of Columbia, and the U.S. territories

g. Supreme audit institutions: national government audit organizations, in the United States or elsewhere, typically headed by a comptroller general or auditor general

Types of GAGAS Engagements

1.13 This section describes the types of engagements that audit organizations may conduct in accordance with GAGAS. This description is not intended to limit or require the types of engagements that may be conducted in accordance with GAGAS.

1.14 All GAGAS engagements begin with objectives, and those objectives determine the type of engagement to be conducted and the applicable standards to be followed. This document classifies financial audits, attestation engagements, reviews of financial statements, and performance audits, as defined by their objectives, as the types of engagements that are covered by GAGAS.

1.15 In some GAGAS engagements, the standards applicable to the specific objective will be apparent. For example, if the objective is to express an opinion on financial statements, the standards for financial audits apply. However, some engagements may have objectives that could be met using more than one approach. For example, if the objective is to determine the reliability of performance measures, auditors can perform this work in accordance with either the standards for attestation engagements or performance audits.

1.16 GAGAS requirements and guidance apply to the types of engagements that auditors may conduct in accordance with GAGAS as follows:

  a. Financial audits: the requirements and guidance in chapters 1 through 6 apply.

  b. Attestation-level examination, review, and agreed-upon procedures engagements and reviews of financial statements: the requirements and guidance in chapters 1 through 5 and 7 apply.

  c. Performance audits: the requirements and guidance in chapters 1 through 5, 8, and 9 apply.

Financial Audits

1.17 Financial audits provide independent assessments of whether entities' reported financial information (e.g., financial condition, results, and use of resources) is presented fairly, in all material respects, in accordance with recognized criteria. Financial audits conducted in accordance with GAGAS include financial statement audits and other related financial audits.

Chapter 1: Foundation and Principles for the Use and Application of Government Auditing Standards

    a. Financial statement audits: The primary purpose of a financial statement audit is to provide financial statement users with an opinion by an auditor on whether an entity's financial statements are presented fairly, in all material respects, in accordance with an applicable financial reporting framework. Reporting on financial statement audits conducted in accordance with GAGAS also includes reports on internal control over financial reporting and on compliance with provisions of laws, regulations, contracts, and grant agreements that have a material effect on the financial statements.

    b. Other types of financial audits: Other types of financial audits conducted in accordance with GAGAS entail various scopes of work, including

        (1) obtaining sufficient, appropriate evidence to form an opinion on a single financial statement or specified elements, accounts, or line items of a financial statement;[1]

        (2) issuing letters (commonly referred to as comfort letters) for underwriters and certain other requesting parties;[2]

        (3) auditing applicable compliance and internal control requirements relating to one or more government programs;[3] and

        (4) conducting an audit of internal control over financial reporting that is integrated with an audit of financial statements (integrated audit).[4]

---

[1] See AU-C section 805, *Special Considerations – Audits of Single Financial Statements and Specific Elements, Accounts, or Items of a Financial Statement* (AICPA, *Professional Standards*).

[2] See AU-C section 920, *Letters for Underwriters and Certain Other Requesting Parties* (AICPA, *Professional Standards*).

[3] See AU-C section 935, *Compliance Audits* (AICPA, *Professional Standards*).

[4] See AU-C section 940, *An Audit of Internal Control Over Financial Reporting That Is Integrated With an Audit of Financial Statements* (AICPA, *Professional Standards*).

Attestation Engagements and Reviews of Financial Statements

1.18 Attestation engagements can cover a broad range of financial or nonfinancial objectives about the subject matter or assertion depending on the users' needs. In an attestation engagement, the subject matter or an assertion by a party other than the auditors is measured or evaluated in accordance with suitable criteria. The work the auditors perform and the level of assurance associated with the report vary based on the type of attestation engagement. The three types of attestation engagements are as follows:

a. Examination: An auditor obtains reasonable assurance by obtaining sufficient, appropriate evidence about the measurement or evaluation of subject matter against criteria in order to be able to draw reasonable conclusions on which to base the auditor's opinion about whether the subject matter is in accordance with (or based on) the criteria or the assertion is fairly stated, in all material respects. The auditor obtains the same level of assurance in an examination as in a financial statement audit.[5]

b. Review: An auditor obtains limited assurance by obtaining sufficient, appropriate review evidence about the measurement or evaluation of subject matter against criteria in order to express a conclusion about whether any material modification should be made to the subject matter in order for it to be in accordance with (or based on) the criteria or to the assertion in order for it to be fairly stated. Review-level work does not include reporting on internal control or compliance with provisions of laws, regulations, contracts, and grant agreements. The auditor obtains the same level of assurance in a review engagement as in a review of financial statements.[6]

c. Agreed-upon procedures engagement: An auditor performs specific procedures on subject matter or an assertion and reports the findings without providing an opinion or a conclusion on it. The specified parties to the engagement agree upon and are responsible for the sufficiency of the procedures for their

---

[5]See AT-C section 205, *Examination Engagements* (AICPA, *Professional Standards*).

[6]See AT-C section 210, *Review Engagements* (AICPA, *Professional Standards*).

Chapter 1: Foundation and Principles for the Use and Application of Government Auditing Standards

purposes. The specified parties are the intended users to whom use of the report is limited.[7]

1.19 The subject matter of an attestation engagement may take many forms, including the following:

a. historical or prospective performance or condition, historical or prospective financial information, performance measurements, or backlog data;

b. physical characteristics, for example, narrative descriptions or square footage of facilities;

c. historical events, for example, the price of a market basket of goods on a certain date;

d. analyses, for example, break-even analyses;

e. systems and processes, for example, internal control; and

f. behavior, for example, corporate governance, compliance with laws and regulations, and human resource practices.

1.20 The objective of the auditor when performing a review of financial statements is to obtain limited assurance as a basis for reporting whether the auditor is aware of any material modifications that should be made to financial statements in order for the financial statements to be in accordance with the applicable financial reporting framework. A review of financial statements does not include obtaining an understanding of the entity's internal control, assessing fraud risk, or certain other procedures ordinarily performed in an audit.[8]

Performance Audits

1.21 Performance audits provide objective analysis, findings, and conclusions to assist management and those charged with governance and oversight with, among other things, improving program performance and operations, reducing costs, facilitating decision making by parties

---

[7]See AT-C section 215, *Agreed-Upon Procedures Engagements* (AICPA, *Professional Standards*).

[8]See AR-C section 90, *Review of Financial Statements* (AICPA, *Professional Standards*).

Chapter 1: Foundation and Principles for the Use and Application of Government Auditing Standards

responsible for overseeing or initiating corrective action, and contributing to public accountability.

1.22 Performance audit objectives vary widely and include assessments of program effectiveness, economy, and efficiency; internal control; compliance; and prospective analyses. Audit objectives may also pertain to the current status or condition of a program. These overall objectives are not mutually exclusive. For example, a performance audit with an objective of determining or evaluating program effectiveness may also involve an additional objective of evaluating the program's internal controls. Key categories of performance audit objectives include the following:

   a. Program effectiveness and results audit objectives. These are frequently interrelated with economy and efficiency objectives. Audit objectives that focus on program effectiveness and results typically measure the extent to which a program is achieving its goals and objectives. Audit objectives that focus on economy and efficiency address the costs and resources used to achieve program results.

   b. Internal control audit objectives. These relate to an assessment of one or more aspects of an entity's system of internal control that is designed to provide reasonable assurance of achieving effective and efficient operations, reliability of reporting for internal and external use, or compliance with provisions of applicable laws and regulations. Internal control objectives also may be relevant when determining the cause of unsatisfactory program performance. Internal control is a process effected by an entity's oversight body, management, and other personnel that provides reasonable assurance that the objectives of an entity will be achieved. Internal control comprises the plans, methods, policies, and procedures used to fulfill the mission, strategic plan, goals, and objectives of the entity.

   c. Compliance audit objectives. These relate to an assessment of compliance with criteria established by provisions of laws, regulations, contracts, and grant agreements, or other requirements that could affect the acquisition, protection, use, and disposition of the entity's resources and the quantity, quality, timeliness, and cost of services the entity produces and delivers. Compliance requirements can be either financial or nonfinancial.

Chapter 1: Foundation and Principles for the Use and Application of Government Auditing Standards

    d. Prospective analysis audit objectives. These provide analysis or conclusions about information that is based on assumptions about events that may occur in the future, along with possible actions that the entity may take in response to the future events.

1.23 Examples of program effectiveness and results audit objectives include

    a. assessing the extent to which legislative, regulatory, or organizational goals and objectives are being achieved;

    b. assessing the relative ability of alternative approaches to yield better program performance or eliminate factors that inhibit program effectiveness;

    c. analyzing the relative cost-effectiveness of a program or activity, focusing on combining cost information or other inputs with (1) information about outputs or the benefit provided or (2) outcomes or the results achieved;

    d. determining whether a program produced intended results or produced results that were not consistent with the program's objectives;

    e. determining the current status or condition of program operations or progress in implementing legislative requirements;

    f. determining whether a program provides access to or distribution of public resources within the context of statutory parameters;

    g. assessing the extent to which programs duplicate, overlap, or conflict with other related programs;

    h. evaluating whether the entity is following sound procurement practices;

    i. assessing the reliability, validity, or relevance of performance measures concerning program effectiveness and results or economy and efficiency;

    j. assessing the reliability, validity, or relevance of financial information related to the performance of a program;

k. determining whether government resources (inputs) are obtained at reasonable costs while meeting timeliness and quality considerations;

l. determining whether appropriate value was obtained based on the cost or amount paid or based on the amount of revenue received;

m. determining whether government services and benefits are accessible to those individuals who have a right to access those services and benefits;

n. determining whether fees assessed cover costs;

o. determining whether and how the program's unit costs can be decreased or its productivity increased; and

p. assessing the reliability, validity, or relevance of budget proposals or budget requests to assist legislatures in the budget process.

1.24 Examples of internal control audit objectives include determining whether

a. organizational missions, goals, and objectives are achieved effectively and efficiently;

b. resources are used in compliance with laws, regulations, or other requirements;

c. resources, including sensitive information accessed or stored outside the organization's physical perimeter, are safeguarded against unauthorized acquisition, use, or disposition;

d. management information, such as performance measures, and public reports are complete, accurate, and consistent to support performance and decision making;

e. the integrity of information from computerized systems is achieved; and

f. contingency planning for information systems provides essential backup to prevent unwarranted disruption of the activities and functions that the systems support.

1.25 Examples of compliance objectives include determining whether

   a. the purpose of the program, the manner in which it is to be conducted, the services delivered, the outcomes, or the population it serves is in compliance with provisions of laws, regulations, contracts, or grant agreements or other requirements;

   b. government services and benefits are distributed or delivered to citizens based on eligibility to obtain those services and benefits;

   c. incurred or proposed costs are in compliance with applicable laws, regulations, contracts, or grant agreements; and

   d. revenues received are in compliance with applicable laws, regulations, contracts, or grant agreements.

1.26 Examples of prospective analysis objectives include providing conclusions based on

   a. current and projected trends and future potential impact on government programs and services and their implications for program or policy alternatives;

   b. program or policy alternatives, including forecasting program outcomes under various assumptions;

   c. policy or legislative proposals, including advantages, disadvantages, and analysis of stakeholder views;

   d. prospective information prepared by management;

   e. budgets and forecasts that are based on (1) assumptions about expected future events and (2) stakeholders' and management's expected reaction to those future events; and

   f. management's assumptions on which prospective information is based.

Terms Used in GAGAS

1.27 This paragraph describes certain terms used in GAGAS. When terminology differs from that used at an organization subject to GAGAS, auditors use professional judgment to determine if there is an equivalent term.[9]

    a. Attestation engagement: An examination, review, or agreed-upon procedures engagement conducted under the GAGAS attestation standards related to subject matter or an assertion that is the responsibility of another party.

    b. Audit: Either a financial audit or performance audit conducted in accordance with GAGAS.

    c. Audit organization: A government audit entity or a public accounting firm or other audit entity that conducts GAGAS engagements.

    d. Audit report: A report issued as a result of a financial audit, attestation engagement, review of financial statements, or performance audit conducted in accordance with GAGAS.

    e. Audited entity: The entity that is subject to a GAGAS engagement, whether that engagement is a financial audit, attestation engagement, review of financial statements, or performance audit.

    f. Auditor: An individual assigned to planning, directing, performing engagement procedures, or reporting on GAGAS engagements (including work on audits, attestation engagements, and reviews of financial statements) regardless of job title. Therefore, individuals who may have the title auditor, information technology auditor, analyst, practitioner, evaluator, inspector, or other similar titles are considered auditors under GAGAS.

    g. Control objective: The aim or purpose of specified controls; control objectives address the risks related to achieving an entity's objectives.

---

[9]See the Glossary for an expanded list of terms used in GAGAS.

h. Engagement: A financial audit, attestation engagement, review of financial statements, or performance audit conducted in accordance with GAGAS.

i. Engagement team (or audit team): Auditors assigned to planning, directing, performing engagement procedures, or reporting on GAGAS engagements.

j. Engaging party: The party that engages the auditor to conduct the GAGAS engagement.

k. Entity objective: What an entity wants to achieve; entity objectives are intended to meet the entity's mission, strategic plan, and goals and the requirements of applicable laws and regulations.

l. External audit organization: An audit organization that issues reports to third parties external to the audited entity, either exclusively or in addition to issuing reports to senior management and those charged with governance of the audited entity.

m. Internal audit organization: An audit organization that is accountable to senior management and those charged with governance of the audited entity and that does not generally issue reports to third parties external to the audited entity.

n. Responsible party: The party responsible for a GAGAS engagement's subject matter.

o. Review of financial statements: An engagement conducted under GAGAS for review of financial statements.

p. Specialist: An individual or organization possessing special skill or knowledge in a particular field other than accounting or auditing that assists auditors in conducting engagements. A specialist may be either an internal specialist or an external specialist.

The GAGAS Format

1.28 GAGAS uses a format designed to allow auditors to quickly identify requirements and application guidance related to those requirements. GAGAS requirements are differentiated from application guidance by borders surrounding the text. The requirements are followed immediately by application guidance that relates directly to the preceding requirements. The auditors' responsibilities related to requirements and application guidance are discussed in paragraphs 2.02 through 2.10.

Chapter 2: General Requirements for Complying with Government Auditing Standards

2.01 This chapter establishes general requirements for complying with generally accepted government auditing standards (GAGAS) that are applicable to all GAGAS engagements. The information it contains relates to how auditors conducting GAGAS engagements identify and apply the requirements contained in GAGAS. The chapter also contains requirements for using other audit standards in conjunction with GAGAS and for reporting compliance with GAGAS in the audit report.

Complying with GAGAS

Requirements: Complying with GAGAS

2.02 GAGAS uses two categories of requirements, identified by specific terms, to describe the degree of responsibility they impose on auditors and audit organizations:

a. Unconditional requirements: Auditors and audit organizations must comply with an unconditional requirement in all cases where such requirement is relevant. GAGAS uses *must* to indicate an unconditional requirement.

b. Presumptively mandatory requirements: Auditors and audit organizations must comply with a presumptively mandatory requirement in all cases where such a requirement is relevant except in rare circumstances discussed in paragraphs 2.03, 2.04, and 2.08. GAGAS uses *should* to indicate a presumptively mandatory requirement.[10]

2.03 In rare circumstances, auditors and audit organizations may determine it necessary to depart from a relevant presumptively mandatory requirement. In such rare circumstances, auditors should perform alternative procedures to achieve the intent of that requirement.

2.04 If, in rare circumstances, auditors judge it necessary to depart from a relevant presumptively mandatory requirement, they must document their justification for the departure and how the alternative

---

[10]See para. 2.19 for additional documentation requirements for departures from GAGAS requirements.

procedures performed in the circumstances were sufficient to achieve the intent of that requirement.

2.05 Auditors should have an understanding of the entire text of applicable chapters of GAGAS, including application guidance, and any amendments that GAO issued, to understand the intent of the requirements and to apply the requirements properly.[11]

2.06 Auditors should consider applicable GAO-issued GAGAS interpretive guidance in conducting and reporting on GAGAS engagements.[12]

Application Guidance: Complying with GAGAS

2.07 GAGAS contains requirements together with related explanatory material in the form of application guidance. Not every paragraph of GAGAS carries a requirement. Rather, GAGAS identifies the requirements through use of specific language. GAGAS also contains introductory material that provides context relevant to a proper understanding of a GAGAS chapter or section. Having an understanding of the entire text of applicable GAGAS includes an understanding of any financial audit, attestation, and reviews of financial statement standards incorporated by reference.[13]

2.08 The need for auditors to depart from a relevant presumptively mandatory requirement is expected to arise only when the requirement is for a specific procedure to be performed and, in the specific circumstances of the engagement, that procedure would be ineffective in achieving the intent of the requirement.

2.09 The application guidance provides further explanation of the requirements and guidance for applying them. In particular, it may explain more precisely what a requirement means or is intended to address or include examples of procedures that may be appropriate in the circumstances. Although such guidance does not in itself impose a

---

[11]See http://www.gao.gov/yellowbook for GAGAS amendments.

[12]See http://www.gao.gov/yellowbook for GAGAS interpretive guidance.

[13]See paras. 2.13, 6.01, and 7.01 for discussion of standards incorporated by reference.

requirement, it is relevant to the proper application of the requirements. "May," "might," and "could" are used to describe these actions and procedures. The application guidance may also provide background information on matters addressed in GAGAS.

2.10 Interpretive guidance is not auditing standards. Interpretive guidance provides guidance on the application of GAGAS and recommendations on the application of GAGAS in specific circumstances.

Relationship between GAGAS and Other Professional Standards

Requirement: Relationship between GAGAS and Other Professional Standards

2.11 When auditors cite compliance with both GAGAS and another set of standards, such as those listed in paragraphs 2.13, 2.15, 6.01, and 7.01, auditors should refer to paragraph 2.17 for the requirements for citing compliance with GAGAS. In addition to citing GAGAS, auditors may also cite the use of other standards in their reports when they have also met the requirements for citing compliance with the other standards. Auditors should refer to the other set of standards for the basis for citing compliance with those standards.

Application Guidance: Relationship between GAGAS and Other Professional Standards

2.12 Auditors may use GAGAS in conjunction with professional standards issued by other authoritative bodies.

2.13 The relationship between GAGAS and other professional standards for financial audits, attestation engagements, and reviews of financial statements is as follows:

a. The American Institute of Certified Public Accountants (AICPA) has established professional standards that apply to financial audits, attestation engagements, and reviews of financial statements for nonissuers (entities other than issuers under the Sarbanes-Oxley Act of 2002,[14] such as privately held companies,

---

[14] See the Sarbanes-Oxley Act of 2002 (Public Law 107-204) for a discussion of issuers (generally, publicly traded companies with a reporting obligation under the Securities Exchange Act of 1934).

nonprofit entities, and government entities) conducted by certified public accountants (CPA). For financial audits and attestation engagements, GAGAS incorporates by reference AICPA Statements on Auditing Standards and Statements on Standards for Attestation Engagements.[15] For reviews of financial statements, GAGAS incorporates by reference AR-C, section 90, *Review of Financial Statements*.[16]

b. The International Auditing and Assurance Standards Board (IAASB) has established professional standards that apply to financial audits and assurance engagements. Auditors may elect to use the IAASB standards and the related International Standards on Auditing and International Standards on Assurance Engagements in conjunction with GAGAS.

c. The Public Company Accounting Oversight Board (PCAOB) has established professional standards that apply to financial audits and attestation engagements for issuers. Auditors may elect to use the PCAOB standards in conjunction with GAGAS.

2.14 For financial audits, attestation engagements, and reviews of financial statements, GAGAS does not incorporate the AICPA Code of Professional Conduct by reference, but recognizes that certain CPAs may use or may be required to use the code in conjunction with GAGAS.

2.15 For performance audits, GAGAS does not incorporate other standards by reference, but recognizes that auditors may use or may be required to use other professional standards in conjunction with GAGAS, such as the following:

a. *International Standards for the Professional Practice of Internal Auditing*, Institute of Internal Auditors, Inc.;

b. *International Standards of Supreme Audit Institutions*, International Organization of Supreme Audit Institutions;

c. *Guiding Principles for Evaluators*, American Evaluation Association;

---

[15]AICPA, *Professional Standards*.

[16]AICPA, *Professional Standards*.

d. *The Program Evaluation Standards*, Joint Committee on Standards for Education Evaluation;

e. *Standards for Educational and Psychological Testing*, American Psychological Association; and

f. *IT Standards, Guidelines, and Tools and Techniques for Audit and Assurance and Control Professionals*, Information Systems Audit and Control Association.

Stating Compliance with GAGAS in the Audit Report

Requirements: Stating Compliance with GAGAS in the Audit Report

2.16 When auditors are required to conduct an engagement in accordance with GAGAS or are representing to others that they did so, they should cite compliance with GAGAS in the audit report as set forth in paragraphs 2.17 through 2.19.

2.17 Auditors should include one of the following types of GAGAS compliance statements in reports on GAGAS engagements, as appropriate.

    a. Unmodified GAGAS compliance statement: Stating that the auditors conducted the engagement in accordance with GAGAS. Auditors should include an unmodified GAGAS compliance statement in the audit report when they have (1) followed unconditional and applicable presumptively mandatory GAGAS requirements or (2) followed unconditional requirements, documented justification for any departures from applicable presumptively mandatory requirements, and achieved the objectives of those requirements through other means.

    b. Modified GAGAS compliance statement: Stating either that

        (1) the auditors conducted the engagement in accordance with GAGAS, except for specific applicable requirements that were not followed, or

        (2) because of the significance of the departure(s) from the

requirements, the auditors were unable to and did not conduct the engagement in accordance with GAGAS.

2.18 When auditors use a modified GAGAS statement, they should disclose in the report the applicable requirement(s) not followed, the reasons for not following the requirement(s), and how not following the requirement(s) affected or could have affected the engagement and the assurance provided.

2.19 When auditors do not comply with applicable requirement(s), they should (1) assess the significance of the noncompliance to the engagement objectives; (2) document the assessment, along with their reasons for not following the requirement(s); and (3) determine the type of GAGAS compliance statement.

Application Guidance: Stating Compliance with GAGAS in the Audit Report

2.20 Situations for using modified compliance statements include scope limitations, such as restrictions on access to records, government officials, or other individuals needed to conduct the engagement.

2.21 The auditors' determination of noncompliance with applicable requirements is a matter of professional judgment, which is affected by the significance of the requirement(s) not followed in relation to the engagement objectives.

2.22 Determining whether an unmodified or modified GAGAS compliance statement is appropriate is based on the consideration of the individual and aggregate effect of the instances of noncompliance with GAGAS requirements. Factors that the auditor may consider include

   a. the pervasiveness of the instance(s) of noncompliance;

   b. the potential effect of the instance(s) of noncompliance on the sufficiency and appropriateness of evidence supporting the findings, conclusions, and recommendations; and

   c. whether report users might misunderstand the implications of a modified or unmodified GAGAS compliance statement.

Chapter 2: General Requirements for Complying with Government Auditing Standards

2.23 If an audit report is issued in situations described in paragraph 3.60 (except in circumstances discussed in paragraphs 3.25 or 3.84), a modified GAGAS compliance statement as discussed in paragraph 2.17b(2) is used.

Chapter 3: Ethics, Independence, and Professional Judgment

3.01 The first section of this chapter sets forth fundamental ethical principles for auditors in the government environment. The second section establishes independence standards and provides guidance on this topic for auditors conducting financial audits, attestation engagements, reviews of financial statements, and performance audits under generally accepted government auditing standards (GAGAS). This section emphasizes the importance of independence of the auditor and the audit organization. The third section establishes the standard for the auditor's use of professional judgment and provides related application guidance. The requirements of this chapter are intended to be followed in conjunction with all other applicable GAGAS requirements.

Ethical Principles

3.02 The ethical principles presented in this section provide the foundation, discipline, and structure, as well as the environment, that influence the application of GAGAS.[17]

3.03 Because auditing is essential to government accountability to the public, the public expects audit organizations and auditors who perform their work in accordance with GAGAS to follow ethical principles. Management of the audit organization sets the tone for ethical behavior throughout the organization by maintaining an ethical culture, clearly communicating acceptable behavior and expectations to each employee, and creating an environment that reinforces and encourages ethical behavior throughout all levels of the organization. The ethical tone maintained and demonstrated by management and personnel is an essential element of a positive ethical environment for the audit organization.

3.04 Performing audit work in accordance with ethical principles is a matter of personal and organizational responsibility. Ethical principles apply in preserving auditor independence,[18] taking on only work that the audit organization is competent to perform,[19] performing high-quality work, and following the applicable standards cited in the audit report. Integrity and objectivity are maintained when auditors perform their work

---

[17]See para. 5.08 for a discussion of ethical requirements in an audit organization's system of quality control.

[18]See paras. 3.18 through 3.108 for requirements and guidance related to independence.

[19]See paras. 4.02 through 4.15 for additional information on competence.

and make decisions that are consistent with the broader interest of those relying on the audit report, including the public.

3.05 Other ethical requirements or codes of professional conduct may also be applicable to auditors who conduct engagements in accordance with GAGAS. For example, individual auditors who are members of professional organizations or are licensed or certified professionals may also be subject to ethical requirements of those professional organizations or licensing bodies. Auditors employed by government entities may also be subject to government ethics laws and regulations.

3.06 The ethical principles that guide the work of auditors who conduct engagements in accordance with GAGAS are

    a. the public interest;

    b. integrity;

    c. objectivity;

    d. proper use of government information, resources, and positions; and

    e. professional behavior.

The Public Interest

3.07 The public interest is defined as the collective well-being of the community of people and entities that the auditors serve. Observing integrity, objectivity, and independence in discharging their professional responsibilities helps auditors serve the public interest and honor the public trust. The principle of the public interest is fundamental to the responsibilities of auditors and critical in the government environment.

3.08 A distinguishing mark of an auditor is acceptance of responsibility to serve the public interest. This responsibility is critical when auditing in the government environment. GAGAS embodies the concept of accountability for public resources, which is fundamental to serving the public interest.

Integrity

3.09 Public confidence in government is maintained and strengthened by auditors performing their professional responsibilities with integrity. Integrity includes auditors performing their work with an attitude that is objective, fact-based, nonpartisan, and nonideological with regard to

Chapter 3: Ethics, Independence, and Professional Judgment

audited entities and users of the audit reports. Within the constraints of applicable confidentiality laws, regulations, or policies, communications with the audited entity, those charged with governance, and the individuals contracting for or requesting the engagement are expected to be honest, candid, and constructive.

3.10 Making decisions consistent with the public interest of the program or activity under audit is an important part of the principle of integrity. In discharging their professional responsibilities, auditors may encounter conflicting pressures from management of the audited entity, various levels of government, and other likely users. Auditors may also encounter pressures to inappropriately achieve personal or organizational gain. In resolving those conflicts and pressures, acting with integrity means that auditors place priority on their responsibilities to the public interest.

Objectivity

3.11 Auditors' objectivity in discharging their professional responsibilities is the basis for the credibility of auditing in the government sector. Objectivity includes independence of mind and appearance when conducting engagements, maintaining an attitude of impartiality, having intellectual honesty, and being free of conflicts of interest. Maintaining objectivity includes a continuing assessment of relationships with audited entities and other stakeholders in the context of the auditors' responsibility to the public. The concepts of objectivity and independence are closely related. Independence impairments affect auditors' objectivity.[20]

Proper Use of Government Information, Resources, and Positions

3.12 Government information, resources, and positions are to be used for official purposes and not inappropriately for the auditors' personal gain or in a manner contrary to law or detrimental to the legitimate interests of the audited entity or the audit organization. This concept includes the proper handling of sensitive or classified information or resources.

3.13 In the government environment, the public's right to the transparency of government information has to be balanced with the proper use of that information. In addition, many government programs are subject to laws and regulations dealing with the disclosure of information. Exercising discretion in using information acquired in the course of auditors' duties is

---

[20]See paras. 3.18 through 3.108 for independence requirements and guidance.

an important part in achieving this balance. Improperly disclosing any such information to third parties is not an acceptable practice.

3.14 Accountability to the public for the proper use and prudent management of government resources is an essential part of auditors' responsibilities. Protecting and conserving government resources and using them appropriately for authorized activities are important elements of the public's expectations for auditors.

3.15 Misusing the auditor position for financial gain or other benefits violates an auditor's fundamental responsibilities. An auditor's credibility can be damaged by actions that could be perceived by an objective third party with knowledge of the relevant information as improperly benefiting an auditor's personal financial interests or those of an immediate or close family member; a general partner; an entity for which the auditor serves as an officer, director, trustee, or employee; or an entity with which the auditor is negotiating concerning future employment.

Professional Behavior

3.16 High expectations for the auditing profession include complying with all relevant legal, regulatory, and professional obligations and avoiding any conduct that could bring discredit to auditors' work, including actions that would cause an objective third party with knowledge of the relevant information to conclude that the auditors' work was professionally deficient. Professional behavior includes auditors putting forth an honest effort in performing their duties in accordance with the relevant technical and professional standards.

Independence

3.17 GAGAS's practical consideration of independence consists of four interrelated sections, providing

    a. general requirements and application guidance;

    b. requirements for and guidance on a conceptual framework for making independence determinations based on facts and circumstances that are often unique to specific environments;

    c. requirements for and guidance on independence for auditors providing nonaudit services, including identification of specific nonaudit services that always impair independence and others that would not normally impair independence; and

d. requirements for and guidance on documentation necessary to support adequate consideration of auditor independence.

> **Requirements: General**
>
> **3.18** In all matters relating to the GAGAS engagement, auditors and audit organizations must be independent from an audited entity.
>
> **3.19** Auditors and audit organizations should avoid situations that could lead reasonable and informed third parties to conclude that the auditors and audit organizations are not independent and thus are not capable of exercising objective and impartial judgment on all issues associated with conducting the engagement and reporting on the work.
>
> **3.20** Except under the limited circumstances discussed in paragraphs 3.66 and 3.67, auditors and audit organizations should be independent from an audited entity during
>
> a. any period of time that falls within the period covered by the financial statements or subject matter of the engagement and
>
> b. the period of professional engagement.

Application Guidance: General

3.21 Independence comprises the following:

a. Independence of mind: The state of mind that permits the conduct of an engagement without being affected by influences that compromise professional judgment, thereby allowing an individual to act with integrity and exercise objectivity and professional skepticism.

b. Independence in appearance: The absence of circumstances that would cause a reasonable and informed third party to reasonably conclude that the integrity, objectivity, or professional skepticism of an audit organization or member of the engagement team had been compromised.

3.22 Auditors and audit organizations maintain their independence so that their opinions, findings, conclusions, judgments, and recommendations will be impartial and will be viewed as impartial by reasonable and informed third parties.

3.23 The period of professional engagement begins when the auditors either sign an initial engagement letter or other agreement to conduct an engagement or begin to conduct an engagement, whichever is earlier. The period lasts for the duration of the professional relationship—which, for recurring engagements, could cover many periods—and ends with the formal or informal notification, either by the auditors or the audited entity, of the termination of the professional relationship or with the issuance of a report, whichever is later. Accordingly, the period of professional engagement does not necessarily end with the issuance of a report and recommence with the beginning of the following year's engagement or a subsequent engagement with a similar objective.

3.24 Under some conditions, the party requesting or requiring an engagement, referred to as the engaging party, will differ from the party responsible for the engagement's subject matter, referred to as the responsible party. Under such conditions, the GAGAS independence requirements apply to the relationship between the auditors and the responsible party, not the relationship between the auditors and the engaging party. The following are examples of conditions under which the party requesting an engagement may differ from the party responsible for the engagement's subject matter.

a. A legislative body requires that auditors conduct, on the legislative body's behalf, a performance audit of program operations that are the responsibility of an executive agency. GAGAS requires that the auditors be independent of the executive agency.

b. A state agency engages an independent public accountant to conduct an examination-level attestation engagement to assess the validity of certain information that a local government provided to the state agency. GAGAS requires that the independent public accountant be independent of the local government.

c. A government department works with a government agency that conducts examination-level attestation engagements of contractor compliance with the terms and conditions of agreements between the department and the contractor. GAGAS requires that the auditors be independent of the contractors.

3.25 Auditors in government sometimes work under conditions that impair independence in accordance with this section. An example of such a circumstance is a threat created by a statutory requirement for auditors to serve in official roles that conflict with the independence requirements of this section, such as a law that requires an auditor to serve as a voting member of an entity's management committee or board of directors, for which there are no safeguards to eliminate or reduce the threats to an acceptable level. Paragraph 2.17b provides standard language for modified GAGAS compliance statements for auditors who experience such impairments. Determining how to modify the GAGAS compliance statement in these circumstances is a matter of professional judgment.

GAGAS Conceptual Framework Approach to Independence

3.26 Many different circumstances, or combinations of circumstances, are relevant in evaluating threats to independence. Therefore, GAGAS establishes a conceptual framework that auditors use to identify, evaluate, and apply safeguards to address threats to independence. The conceptual framework assists auditors in maintaining both independence of mind and independence in appearance. It can be applied to many variations in circumstances that create threats to independence and allows auditors to address threats to independence that result from activities that are not specifically prohibited by GAGAS.

> **Requirements: GAGAS Conceptual Framework Approach to Independence**
>
> **3.27** Auditors should apply the conceptual framework[21] at the audit organization, engagement team, and individual auditor levels to
>
> a. identify threats to independence;
>
> b. evaluate the significance of the threats identified, both individually and in the aggregate; and
>
> c. apply safeguards as necessary to eliminate the threats or reduce them to an acceptable level.
>
> **3.28** Auditors should reevaluate threats to independence, including

---

[21] See fig. 1 at the end of ch. 3 for a flowchart on applying the conceptual framework in accordance with GAGAS.

any safeguards applied, whenever the audit organization or the auditors become aware of new information or changes in facts and circumstances that could affect whether a threat has been eliminated or reduced to an acceptable level.

3.29 Auditors should use professional judgment when applying the conceptual framework.

3.30 Auditors should evaluate the following broad categories of threats to independence when applying the GAGAS conceptual framework:

  a. Self-interest threat: The threat that a financial or other interest will inappropriately influence an auditor's judgment or behavior.

  b. Self-review threat: The threat that an auditor or audit organization that has provided nonaudit services will not appropriately evaluate the results of previous judgments made or services provided as part of the nonaudit services when forming a judgment significant to a GAGAS engagement.

  c. Bias threat: The threat that an auditor will, as a result of political, ideological, social, or other convictions, take a position that is not objective.

  d. Familiarity threat: The threat that aspects of a relationship with management or personnel of an audited entity, such as a close or long relationship, or that of an immediate or close family member, will lead an auditor to take a position that is not objective.

  e. Undue influence threat: The threat that influences or pressures from sources external to the audit organization will affect an auditor's ability to make objective judgments.

  f. Management participation threat: The threat that results from an auditor's taking on the role of management or otherwise performing management functions on behalf of the audited entity, which will lead an auditor to take a position that is not objective.

  g. Structural threat: The threat that an audit organization's placement within a government entity, in combination with the structure of the government entity being audited, will affect the audit organization's ability to perform work and report results objectively.

3.31 Auditors should determine whether identified threats to independence are at an acceptable level or have been eliminated or reduced to an acceptable level, considering both qualitative and quantitative factors to determine the significance of a threat.

3.32 When auditors determine that threats to independence are not at an acceptable level, the auditors should determine whether appropriate safeguards can be applied to eliminate the threats or reduce them to an acceptable level.

3.33 In cases where auditors determine that threats to independence require the application of safeguards, auditors should document the threats identified and the safeguards applied to eliminate or reduce the threats to an acceptable level.

3.34 If auditors initially identify a threat to independence after the audit report is issued, auditors should evaluate the threat's effect on the engagement and on GAGAS compliance. If the auditors determine that the newly identified threat's effect on the engagement would have resulted in the audit report being different from the report issued had the auditors been aware of it, they should communicate in the same manner as that used to originally distribute the report to those charged with governance, the appropriate officials of the audited entity, the appropriate officials of the audit organization requiring or arranging for the engagements, and other known users, so that they do not continue to rely on findings or conclusions that were affected by the threat to independence. If auditors previously posted the report to their publicly accessible website, they should remove the report and post a public notification that the report was removed. The auditors should then determine whether to perform the additional engagement work necessary to reissue the report, including any revised findings or conclusions, or to repost the original report if the additional engagement work does not result in a change in findings or conclusions.

Application Guidance: GAGAS Conceptual Framework Approach to Independence

3.35 For consideration of auditor independence, offices or units of an audit organization, or related or affiliated entities under common control, are not differentiated from one another. Consequently, for the purposes of evaluating independence using the conceptual framework, an audit organization that includes multiple offices or units, or includes multiple entities related or affiliated through common control, is considered to be one audit organization. Common ownership may also affect independence in appearance regardless of the level of control.

Identifying Threats

3.36 Facts and circumstances that create threats to independence can result from events such as the start of a new engagement, assignment of new personnel to an ongoing engagement, and acceptance of a nonaudit service for an audited entity.

3.37 Threats to independence may be created by a wide range of relationships and circumstances. Circumstances that result in a threat to independence in one of the categories may result in other threats as well.

3.38 Examples of circumstances that create self-interest threats for an auditor follow:

   a. An audit organization having undue dependence on income from a particular audited entity.

   b. A member of the audit team entering into employment negotiations with an audited entity.

   c. An audit organization discovering a significant error when evaluating the results of a previous professional service provided by the audit organization.

   d. A member of the audit team having a direct financial interest in the audited entity. However, this would not preclude auditors from auditing pension plans that they participate in if (1) the auditors have no control over the investment strategy, benefits, or other management issues associated with the pension plan and (2) the auditors belong to such pension plan as part of their employment with the audit organization or prior employment with the audited entity, provided that the plan is normally offered to all employees in equivalent employment positions.

3.39 Examples of circumstances that create self-review threats for an auditor follow:

a. An audit organization issuing a report on the effectiveness of the operation of financial or performance management systems after designing or implementing the systems.

b. An audit organization having prepared the original data used to generate records that are the subject matter of the engagement.

c. An audit organization providing a service for an audited entity that directly affects the subject matter information of the engagement.

d. A member of the engagement team being, or having recently been, employed by the audited entity in a position to exert significant influence over the subject matter of the engagement.

3.40 Examples of circumstances that create bias threats for an auditor follow:

a. A member of the engagement team having preconceptions about the objectives of a program under audit that are strong enough to affect the auditor's objectivity.

b. A member of the engagement team having biases associated with political, ideological, or social convictions that result from membership or employment in, or loyalty to, a particular type of policy, group, entity, or level of government that could affect the auditor's objectivity.

3.41 Examples of circumstances that create familiarity threats for an auditor follow:

a. A member of the engagement team having a close or immediate family member who is a principal or senior manager of the audited entity.

b. A member of the engagement team having a close or immediate family member who is an employee of the audited entity and is in a position to exert significant influence over the subject matter of the engagement.

c. A principal or employee of the audited entity having recently served on the engagement team in a position to exert significant influence over the subject matter of the engagement.

d. An auditor accepting gifts or preferential treatment from an audited entity, unless the value is trivial or inconsequential.

e. Senior engagement personnel having a long association with the audited entity.

3.42 Examples of circumstances that create undue influence threats for an auditor or audit organization include existence of the following:

a. External interference or influence that could improperly limit or modify the scope of an engagement or threaten to do so, including exerting pressure to inappropriately reduce the extent of work performed in order to reduce costs or fees.

b. External interference with the selection or application of engagement procedures or in the selection of transactions to be examined.

c. Unreasonable restrictions on the time allowed to complete an engagement or issue the report.

d. External interference over assignment, appointment, compensation, and promotion.

e. Restrictions on funds or other resources provided to the audit organization that adversely affect the audit organization's ability to carry out its responsibilities.

f. Authority to overrule or to inappropriately influence the auditors' judgment as to the appropriate content of the report.

g. Threat of replacing the auditor or the audit organization based on a disagreement with the contents of an audit report, the auditors' conclusions, or the application of an accounting principle or other criteria.

Chapter 3: Ethics, Independence, and
Professional Judgment

h. Influences that jeopardize the auditors' continued employment for reasons other than incompetence, misconduct, or the audited entity's need for GAGAS engagements.

3.43 Examples of circumstances that create management participation threats for an auditor follow:

a. A member of the engagement team being, or having recently been, a principal or senior manager of the audited entity.

b. An auditor serving as a voting member of an entity's management committee or board of directors, making policy decisions that affect future direction and operation of an entity's programs, supervising entity employees, developing or approving programmatic policy, authorizing an entity's transactions, or maintaining custody of an entity's assets.

c. An auditor or audit organization recommending a single individual for a specific position that is key to the audited entity or program under audit, or otherwise ranking or influencing management's selection of the candidate.

d. An auditor preparing management's corrective action plan to deal with deficiencies detected in the engagement.

3.44 Examples of circumstances that create structural threats for an auditor follow:

a. For both external and internal audit organizations, structural placement of the audit function within the reporting line of the areas under audit.

b. For internal audit organizations, administrative direction from the audited entity's management.

Evaluating Threats

3.45 Threats to independence are evaluated both individually and in the aggregate, as threats can have a cumulative effect on auditors' independence.

3.46 When evaluating threats to independence, an acceptable level is a level at which a reasonable and informed third party would likely conclude

Chapter 3: Ethics, Independence, and
Professional Judgment

that the audit organization or auditor is independent. The concept of a reasonable and informed third party is a test that involves an evaluation by a hypothetical person. Such a person possesses skills, knowledge, and experience to objectively evaluate the appropriateness of the auditor's judgments and conclusions. This evaluation entails weighing all the relevant facts and circumstances, including any safeguards applied, that the auditor knows, or could reasonably be expected to know, at the time that the evaluation is made.

3.47 A threat to independence is not at an acceptable level if it either

    a. could affect the auditors' ability to conduct an engagement without being affected by influences that compromise professional judgment or

    b. could expose the auditors or audit organization to circumstances that would cause a reasonable and informed third party to conclude that the integrity, objectivity, or professional skepticism of the audit organization, or an auditor, had been compromised.

3.48 The GAGAS section on nonaudit services in paragraphs 3.64 through 3.106 provides requirements and guidance on evaluating threats to independence related to nonaudit services that auditors provide to audited entities. That section also enumerates specific nonaudit services that always impair auditor independence with respect to audited entities and that auditors are prohibited from providing to audited entities.

Applying Safeguards

3.49 Safeguards are actions or other measures, individually or in combination, that auditors and audit organizations take that effectively eliminate threats to independence or reduce them to an acceptable level. Safeguards vary depending on the facts and circumstances.

3.50 Examples of safeguards include

    a. consulting an independent third party, such as a professional organization, a professional regulatory body, or another auditor to discuss engagement issues or assess issues that are highly technical or that require significant judgment;

    b. involving another audit organization to perform or re-perform part of the engagement;

Chapter 3: Ethics, Independence, and
Professional Judgment

c. having an auditor who was not a member of the engagement team review the work performed; and

d. removing an auditor from an engagement team when that auditor's financial or other interests or relationships pose a threat to independence.

3.51 The lists of safeguards in 3.50 and 3.69 cannot provide safeguards for all circumstances. They may, however, provide a starting point for auditors who have identified threats to independence and are considering what safeguards could eliminate those threats or reduce them to an acceptable level. In some cases, multiple safeguards may be necessary to address a threat.

Audit Organizations in Government Entities

3.52 The ability of an audit organization structurally located in a government entity to perform work and report the results objectively can be affected by its placement within the government entity and the structure of the government entity being audited. The independence standard applies to auditors in both external audit organizations (reporting to third parties externally or to both internal and external parties) and internal audit organizations (reporting only to senior management within the audited entity). Such audit organizations are often subject to constitutional or statutory safeguards that mitigate the effects of structural threats to independence.

3.53 For external audit organizations, constitutional or statutory safeguards that mitigate the effects of structural threats to independence may include governmental structures under which a government audit organization is

a. at a level of government other than the one of which the audited entity is part (federal, state, or local)—for example, federal auditors auditing a state government program—or

b. placed within a different branch of government from that of the audited entity—for example, legislative auditors auditing an executive branch program.

3.54 Safeguards other than those described in paragraph 3.53 may mitigate threats resulting from governmental structures. For external audit organizations, structural threats may be mitigated if the head of the audit

Chapter 3: Ethics, Independence, and
Professional Judgment

organization meets any of the following criteria in accordance with constitutional or statutory requirements:

   a. directly elected by voters of the jurisdiction being audited;

   b. elected or appointed by a legislative body, subject to removal by a legislative body, and reporting the results of engagements to and accountable to a legislative body;

   c. appointed by someone other than a legislative body, so long as the appointment is confirmed by a legislative body and removal from the position is subject to oversight or approval by a legislative body, and reports the results of engagements to and is accountable to a legislative body; or

   d. appointed by, accountable to, reports to, and can only be removed by a statutorily created governing body, the majority of whose members are independently elected or appointed and are outside the organization being audited.

3.55 In addition to the criteria in paragraphs 3.53 and 3.54, GAGAS recognizes that there may be other organizational structures under which external audit organizations in government entities could be considered independent. If appropriately designed and implemented, these structures provide safeguards that prevent the audited entity from interfering with the audit organization's ability to perform the work and report the results impartially. An external audit organization may be structurally independent under a structure different from the ones listed in paragraphs 3.53 and 3.54 if the government audit organization is subject to all of the following constitutional or statutory provisions. The following constitutional or statutory provisions may also be used as safeguards to augment those listed in paragraphs 3.53 and 3.54:

   a. protections that prevent the audited entity from abolishing the audit organization;

   b. protections requiring that if the head of the audit organization is removed from office, the head of the agency reports this fact and the reasons for the removal to the legislative body;

   c. protections that prevent the audited entity from interfering with the initiation, scope, timing, and completion of any engagement;

d. protections that prevent the audited entity from interfering with audit reporting, including the findings and conclusions or the manner, means, or timing of the audit organization's reports;

e. protections that require the audit organization to report to a legislative body or other independent governing body on a recurring basis;

f. protections that give the audit organization sole authority over the selection, retention, advancement, and dismissal of its personnel; and

g. access to records and documents related to the agency, program, or function being audited and access to government officials or other individuals as needed to conduct the engagement.

3.56 Government internal auditors who work under the direction of the audited entity's management are considered structurally independent for the purposes of reporting internally, if the head of the audit organization meets all of the following criteria:

a. is accountable to the head or deputy head of the government entity or to those charged with governance;

b. reports the engagement results both to the head or deputy head of the government entity and to those charged with governance;

c. is located organizationally outside the staff or line management function of the unit under audit;

d. has access to those charged with governance; and

e. is sufficiently removed from pressures to conduct engagements and report findings, opinions, and conclusions objectively without fear of reprisal.

Internal Auditors

3.57 Certain entities employ auditors to work for entity management. These auditors may be subject to administrative direction from persons involved in the entity management process. Such audit organizations are internal audit functions and are encouraged to use the Institute of Internal

Auditors' *International Standards for the Professional Practice of Internal Auditing*, in conjunction with GAGAS.

3.58 When an internal audit organization conducts engagements pertaining to external parties, such as contractors or entities subject to other outside agreements, and no impairments to independence exist, the audit organization can be considered independent as an external audit organization of those external parties.

> **Requirements: Independence Impairments**
>
> **3.59** Auditors should conclude that independence is impaired if no safeguards have been effectively applied to eliminate an unacceptable threat or reduce it to an acceptable level.
>
> **3.60** When auditors conclude that independence of the engagement team or the audit organization is impaired under paragraph 3.59, auditors should decline to accept an engagement or should terminate an engagement in progress (except in circumstances discussed in paragraphs 3.25 or 3.84).

Application Guidance: Independence Impairments

3.61 Whether independence is impaired depends on the nature of the threat, whether the threat is of such significance that it would compromise an auditor's professional judgment or create the appearance that the auditor's integrity, objectivity, or professional skepticism may be compromised, and the specific safeguards applied to eliminate the threat or reduce it to an acceptable level.

3.62 If auditors conclude that an individual auditor's independence is impaired under paragraph 3.59, it may be necessary to terminate the engagement or it may be possible to take action that satisfactorily addresses the effect of the individual auditor's independence impairment.

3.63 Factors that are relevant in evaluating whether the independence of the engagement team or the audit organization is impaired by an individual auditor's independence impairment include

    a. the nature and duration of the individual auditor's impairment;

b. the number and nature of any previous impairments with respect to the current engagement;

c. whether a member of the engagement team had knowledge of the interest or relationship that caused the individual auditor's impairment;

d. whether the individual auditor whose independence is impaired is (1) a member of the engagement team or (2) another individual for whom there are independence requirements;

e. the role of the individual auditor on the engagement team whose independence is impaired;

f. the effect of the service, if any, on the accounting records or audited entity's financial statements if the individual auditor's impairment was caused by the provision of a nonaudit service;

g. whether a partner or director of the audit organization had knowledge of the individual auditor's impairment and failed to ensure that the individual auditor's impairment was promptly communicated to an appropriate individual within the audit organization; and

h. the extent of the self-interest, undue influence, or other threats created by the individual auditor's impairment.

Provision of Nonaudit Services to Audited Entities

Requirement: Nonaudit Services

3.64 Before auditors agree to provide a nonaudit service to an audited entity, they should determine whether providing such a service would create a threat to independence, either by itself or in aggregate with other nonaudit services provided, with respect to any GAGAS engagement they conduct.

Application Guidance: Nonaudit Services

3.65 Auditors have traditionally provided a range of nonaudit services that are consistent with their skills and expertise. Providing nonaudit services to audited entities may create threats to the independence of auditors or audit organizations.

Chapter 3: Ethics, Independence, and
Professional Judgment

3.66 For performance audits and agreed-upon procedures engagements, nonaudit services that are otherwise prohibited by GAGAS may be provided when such services do not relate to the specific subject matter of the engagement.

3.67 For financial audits, examination or review engagements, and reviews of financial statements, a nonaudit service otherwise prohibited by GAGAS and provided during the period covered by the financial statements may not threaten independence with respect to those financial statements provided that the following conditions exist:

   a. the nonaudit service was provided prior to the period of professional engagement;

   b. the nonaudit service related only to periods prior to the period covered by the financial statements; and

   c. the financial statements for the period to which the nonaudit service did relate were audited by other auditors (or in the case of an examination, review, or review of financial statements, examined, reviewed, or audited by other auditors as appropriate).

3.68 Nonaudit services that auditors provide can affect independence of mind and in appearance in periods after the nonaudit services were provided. For example, if auditors have designed and implemented an accounting and financial reporting system that is expected to be in place for many years, a threat to independence in appearance may exist in subsequent periods for future engagements that those auditors conduct. For recurring engagements, having another independent audit organization conduct an engagement over the areas affected by the nonaudit service may provide a safeguard that allows the audit organization that provided the nonaudit service to mitigate the threat to its independence.

3.69 The following are examples of actions that in certain circumstances could be safeguards in addressing threats to independence related to nonaudit services:

   a. not including individuals who provided the nonaudit service as engagement team members;

   b. having another auditor, not associated with the engagement, review the engagement and nonaudit work as appropriate;

Chapter 3: Ethics, Independence, and
Professional Judgment

c. engaging another audit organization to evaluate the results of the nonaudit service; or

d. having another audit organization re-perform the nonaudit service to the extent necessary to enable that other audit organization to take responsibility for the service.

Routine Activities

3.70 Routine activities that auditors perform related directly to conducting an engagement, such as providing advice and responding to questions as part of an engagement, are not considered nonaudit services under GAGAS. Such routine activities generally involve providing advice or assistance to the audited entity on an informal basis as part of an engagement. Routine activities typically are insignificant in terms of time incurred or resources expended and generally do not result in a specific project or engagement or in the auditors producing a formal report or other formal work product. However, activities such as financial statement preparation, cash-to-accrual conversions, and reconciliations are considered nonaudit services under GAGAS, not routine activities related to the performance of an engagement, and are evaluated using the conceptual framework as discussed in paragraphs 3.87 through 3.95.

3.71 Routine activities directly related to an engagement may include the following:

a. providing advice to the audited entity on an accounting matter as an ancillary part of the overall financial audit;

b. providing advice to the audited entity on routine business matters;

c. educating the audited entity about matters within the technical expertise of the auditors; and

d. providing information to the audited entity that is readily available to the auditors, such as best practices and benchmarking studies.

Other Services Provided by Government Audit Organizations

3.72 Audit organizations in government entities frequently provide services that differ from the traditional professional services that an accounting or consulting firm provides to or for an audited entity. These types of services are often provided in response to a statutory

Chapter 3: Ethics, Independence, and
Professional Judgment

requirement, at the discretion of the authority of the audit organization, or to an engaging party (such as a legislative oversight body or an independent external organization) rather than a responsible party, and would generally not create a threat to independence. Examples of these types of services include the following:

a. providing information or data to a requesting party without auditor evaluation or verification of the information or data;

b. developing standards, methodologies, audit guides, audit programs, or criteria for use throughout the government or for use in certain specified situations;

c. collaborating with other professional organizations to advance auditing of government entities and programs;

d. developing question and answer documents to promote understanding of technical issues or standards;

e. providing assistance and technical expertise to legislative bodies or independent external organizations;

f. assisting legislative bodies by developing questions for use at hearings;

g. providing training, speeches, and technical presentations;

h. providing assistance in reviewing budget submissions;

i. contracting for audit services on behalf of an audited entity and overseeing the audit contract, as long as the overarching principles are not violated and the auditor under contract reports to the audit organization and not to management; and

j. providing audit, investigative, and oversight-related services that do not involve a GAGAS engagement, such as

(1) investigations of alleged fraud, violation of contract provisions or grant agreements, or abuse;

(2) periodic audit recommendation follow-up engagements and reports; and

(3) identifying best practices or leading practices for use in advancing the practices of government organizations.

> **Requirements: Management Responsibilities**
>
> **3.73** Before auditors agree to provide nonaudit services to an audited entity that the audited entity's management requested and that could create a threat to independence, either by themselves or in aggregate with other nonaudit services provided, with respect to any GAGAS engagement they conduct, auditors should determine that the audited entity has designated an individual who possesses suitable skill, knowledge, or experience and that the individual understands the services to be provided sufficiently to oversee them.
>
> **3.74** Auditors should document consideration of management's ability to effectively oversee nonaudit services to be provided.
>
> **3.75** In cases where the audited entity is unable or unwilling to assume these responsibilities (for example, the audited entity does not have an individual with suitable skill, knowledge, or experience to oversee the nonaudit services provided, or is unwilling to perform such functions because of lack of time or desire), auditors should conclude that the provision of these services is an impairment to independence.
>
> **3.76** Auditors providing nonaudit services to audited entities should obtain agreement from audited entity management that audited entity management performs the following functions in connection with the nonaudit services:
>
> a. assumes all management responsibilities;
>
> b. oversees the services, by designating an individual, preferably within senior management, who possesses suitable skill, knowledge, or experience;
>
> c. evaluates the adequacy and results of the services provided; and
>
> d. accepts responsibility for the results of the services.
>
> **3.77** In connection with nonaudit services, auditors should establish and document their understanding with the audited entity's

management or those charged with governance, as appropriate, regarding the following:

    a. objectives of the nonaudit service,

    b. services to be provided,

    c. audited entity's acceptance of its responsibilities as discussed in paragraph 3.76,

    d. the auditors' responsibilities, and

    e. any limitations on the provision of nonaudit services.

3.78 Auditors should conclude that management responsibilities that the auditors perform for an audited entity are impairments to independence. If the auditors were to assume management responsibilities for an audited entity, the management participation threats created would be so significant that no safeguards could reduce them to an acceptable level.

Application Guidance: Management Responsibilities

3.79 A critical component of determining whether a threat to independence exists is consideration of management's ability to effectively oversee the nonaudit service to be provided. Although the responsible individual in management is required to have sufficient expertise to oversee the nonaudit services, management is not required to possess the expertise to perform or re-perform the services. However, indicators of management's ability to effectively oversee the nonaudit service include management's ability to determine the reasonableness of the results of the nonaudit services provided and to recognize a material error, omission, or misstatement in the results of the nonaudit services provided.

3.80 Management responsibilities involve leading and directing an entity, including making decisions regarding the acquisition, deployment, and control of human, financial, physical, and intangible resources.

3.81 The following are considered management responsibilities:

    a. setting policies and strategic direction for the audited entity;

b. directing and accepting responsibility for the actions of the audited entity's employees in the performance of their routine, recurring activities;

c. having custody of an audited entity's assets;

d. reporting to those charged with governance on behalf of management;

e. deciding which of the audit organization's or outside third party's recommendations to implement;

f. accepting responsibility for the management of an audited entity's project;

g. accepting responsibility for designing, implementing, or maintaining internal control;

h. providing services that are intended to be used as management's primary basis for making decisions that are significant to the subject matter of the engagement;

i. developing an audited entity's performance measurement system when that system is material or significant to the subject matter of the engagement; and

j. serving as a voting member of an audited entity's management committee or board of directors.

3.82 Whether a specific activity is a management responsibility as identified in paragraph 3.81 or otherwise depends on the facts and circumstances.

Requirements: Providing Nonaudit Services

3.83 Auditors who previously provided nonaudit services for an entity that is a prospective subject of an engagement should evaluate the effect of those nonaudit services on independence before agreeing to conduct a GAGAS engagement. If auditors provided a nonaudit service in the period to be covered by the engagement, they should (1) determine if GAGAS expressly prohibits the nonaudit service; (2) if audited entity management requested the nonaudit service, determine whether the skills, knowledge, and experience of the individual responsible for overseeing the nonaudit service were sufficient; and (3) determine whether a threat to independence exists and address any threats noted in accordance with the conceptual framework.

3.84 Auditors in a government entity may be required to provide a nonaudit service that impairs the auditors' independence with respect to a required engagement. If, because of constitutional or statutory requirements over which they have no control, the auditors can neither implement safeguards to reduce the resulting threat to an acceptable level nor decline to provide or terminate a nonaudit service that is incompatible with engagement responsibilities, auditors should disclose the nature of the threat that could not be eliminated or reduced to an acceptable level and modify the GAGAS compliance statement as discussed in paragraph 2.17b accordingly. Determining how to modify the GAGAS compliance statement in these circumstances is a matter of professional judgment.

Consideration of Specific Nonaudit Services

3.85 By their nature, certain nonaudit services directly support an entity's operations and, if provided to an audited entity, create a threat to the auditors' ability to maintain independence in mind and appearance. Some aspects of these services will impair auditors' ability to conduct GAGAS engagements for the entities to which the services are provided.

3.86 Auditors may be able to provide nonaudit services in the broad areas indicated in paragraphs 3.87 through 3.106 without impairing independence if (1) the nonaudit services are not expressly prohibited by GAGAS requirements, (2) the auditors have determined that the requirements for providing nonaudit services in paragraphs 3.73 through 3.78 and paragraph 3.83 have been met, and (3) any significant threats to independence have been eliminated or reduced to an acceptable level through the application of safeguards. The conceptual framework enables auditors to evaluate independence given the facts and circumstances of individual services that are not specifically prohibited.

Requirements: Preparing Accounting Records and Financial Statements

3.87 Auditors should conclude that the following services involving preparation of accounting records impair independence with respect to an audited entity:

a. determining or changing journal entries, account codes or classifications for transactions, or other accounting records for the entity without obtaining management's approval;

b. authorizing or approving the entity's transactions; and

c. preparing or making changes to source documents without management approval.

3.88 Auditors should conclude that preparing financial statements in their entirety from a client-provided trial balance or underlying accounting records creates significant threats to auditors' independence, and should document the threats and safeguards applied to eliminate and reduce threats to an acceptable level in accordance with paragraph 3.33 or decline to provide the services.[22]

3.89 Auditors should identify as threats to independence any services related to preparing accounting records and financial statements, other than those defined as impairments to independence in paragraph 3.87 and significant threats in paragraph 3.88. These services include

a. recording transactions for which management has determined or approved the appropriate account classification, or posting coded transactions to an audited entity's general ledger;

b. preparing certain line items or sections of the financial statements based on information in the trial balance;

c. posting entries that an audited entity's management has approved to the entity's trial balance; and

---

[22]See fig. 2 at the end of ch. 3 for a flowchart on independence considerations for preparing accounting records and financial statements.

d. preparing account reconciliations that identify reconciling items for the audited entity management's evaluation.

3.90 Auditors should evaluate the significance of threats to independence created by providing any services discussed in paragraph 3.89 and should document the evaluation of the significance of such threats.[23]

Application Guidance: Preparing Accounting Records and Financial Statements

3.91 Management is responsible for the preparation and fair presentation of the financial statements in accordance with the applicable financial reporting framework, even if the auditor assisted in drafting those financial statements. Consequently, an auditor accepting responsibility for the preparation and fair presentation of financial statements that the auditor will subsequently audit or that will otherwise be the subject matter of an engagement would impair the auditor's independence.

3.92 Source documents include those providing evidence that transactions have occurred (for example, purchase orders, payroll time records, customer orders, and contracts). Such records also include an audited entity's general ledger and subsidiary records or equivalent.

3.93 Determining whether services, as discussed in paragraph 3.89, are significant threats and require safeguards is a matter of professional judgment.

3.94 Factors that are relevant in evaluating the significance of any threats created by providing services as discussed in paragraph 3.89 include

a. the extent to which the outcome of the service could have a material effect on the financial statements,

b. the degree of subjectivity involved in determining the appropriate amounts or treatment for those matters reflected in the financial statements, and

---

[23]See para. 3.33 for additional requirements related to documenting threats identified and safeguards applied to eliminate or reduce threats to an acceptable level.

c. the extent of the audited entity's involvement in determining significant matters of judgment.

3.95 Providing clerical assistance, such as typing, formatting, printing, and binding financial statements, is unlikely to be a significant threat.

Requirement: Internal Audit Assistance Services Provided by External Auditors

3.96 Internal audit assistance services involve assisting an entity in performing its internal audit activities. Auditors should conclude that the following internal audit assistance activities impair an external auditor's independence with respect to an audited entity:

a. setting internal audit policies or the strategic direction of internal audit activities;

b. performing procedures that form part of the internal control, such as reviewing and approving changes to employee data access privileges; and

c. determining the scope of the internal audit function and resulting work.

Requirements: Internal Control Evaluation as a Nonaudit Service

3.97 Auditors should conclude that providing or supervising ongoing monitoring procedures over an entity's system of internal control impairs independence because the management participation threat created is so significant that no safeguards could reduce the threat to an acceptable level.

3.98 Separate evaluations are sometimes provided as a nonaudit service. When providing separate evaluations as nonaudit services, auditors should evaluate the significance of the threat created by performing separate evaluations and apply safeguards when necessary to eliminate the threat or reduce it to an acceptable level.

Application Guidance: Internal Control Evaluation as a Nonaudit Service

3.99 Accepting responsibility for designing, implementing, or maintaining internal control includes accepting responsibility for designing, implementing, or maintaining monitoring procedures. Monitoring involves the use of either ongoing monitoring procedures or separate evaluations to gather and analyze persuasive information supporting conclusions about the effectiveness of the internal control system. Ongoing monitoring procedures performed on behalf of management are built into the routine, recurring operating activities of an entity.

3.100 Factors relevant to evaluating the significance of any threats created by providing separate evaluations as a nonaudit service include

a. the frequency of the separate evaluations and

b. the scope or extent of the controls (in relation to the scope of the engagement conducted) being evaluated.

3.101 A separate evaluation provided as a nonaudit service is not a substitute for engagement procedures in a GAGAS engagement.

Requirement: Information Technology Services

3.102 Auditors should conclude that providing information technology (IT) services to an audited entity that relate to the period under audit impairs independence if those services include

a. designing or developing an audited entity's financial information system or other IT system that will play a significant role in the management of an area of operations that is or will be the subject matter of an engagement;

b. making other than insignificant modifications to source code underlying an audited entity's existing financial information system or other IT system that will play a significant role in the management of an area of operations that is or will be the subject matter of an engagement;

> c. supervising audited entity personnel in the daily operation of an audited entity's information system; or
>
> d. operating an audited entity's network, financial information system, or other IT system that will play a significant role in the management of an area of operations that is or will be the subject matter of an engagement.

Application Guidance: Information Technology Services

3.103 Services related to IT systems include the design or implementation of hardware or software systems. The systems may aggregate source data, form part of the internal control over the subject matter of the engagement, or generate information that affects the subject matter of the engagement.

> **Requirement: Appraisal, Valuation, and Actuarial Services**
>
> **3.104** Auditors should conclude that independence is impaired if an audit organization provides appraisal, valuation, or actuarial services to an audited entity when (1) the services involve a significant degree of subjectivity and (2) the results of the service, individually or when combined with other valuation, appraisal, or actuarial services, are material to the audited entity's financial statements or other information on which the audit organization is reporting.

Application Guidance: Appraisal, Valuation, and Actuarial Services

3.105 A valuation comprises the making of assumptions with regard to future developments; the application of appropriate methodologies and techniques; and the combination of both to compute a certain value, or range of values, for an asset, a liability, or an entity as a whole.

Chapter 3: Ethics, Independence, and
Professional Judgment

Requirement: Other Nonaudit Services

3.106 Auditors should conclude that providing certain other nonaudit services impairs an external auditor's independence with respect to an audited entity. These activities include the following:

a. Advisory service

    (1) Assuming any management responsibilities

b. Benefit plan administration

    (1) Making policy decisions on behalf of management

    (2) Interpreting the provisions in a plan document for a plan participant on behalf of management without first obtaining management's concurrence

    (3) Making disbursements on behalf of the plan

    (4) Having custody of the plan's assets

    (5) Serving in a fiduciary capacity, as defined under the Employee Retirement Income Security Act of 1974[24]

c. Business risk consulting

    (1) Making or approving business risk decisions

    (2) Presenting business risk considerations to those charged with governance on behalf of management

d. Executive or employee recruiting

    (1) Committing the audited entity to employee compensation or benefit arrangements

    (2) Hiring or terminating the audited entity's employees

---

[24]See Section 2510.3-21 of Title 29, *Code of Federal Regulations*.

e. Investment advisory or management

   (1) Making investment decisions on behalf of management or otherwise having discretionary authority over an audited entity's investments

   (2) Executing a transaction to buy or sell an audited entity's investments

   (3) Having custody of an audited entity's assets, such as taking temporary possession of securities

Documentation

Requirement: Documentation

3.107 While insufficient documentation of an auditor's compliance with the independence standard does not impair independence, auditors should prepare appropriate documentation under the GAGAS quality control and assurance requirements.[25] The independence standard includes the following documentation requirements, where applicable:

a. document threats to independence that require the application of safeguards, along with safeguards applied, in accordance with the conceptual framework for independence as required by paragraph 3.33;

b. document the safeguards in paragraphs 3.52 through 3.56 if an audit organization is structurally located within a government entity and is considered structurally independent based on those safeguards;

c. document consideration of audited entity management's ability to effectively oversee a nonaudit service to be provided by the auditor as indicated in paragraph 3.74;

---

[25]See para. 5.04 for additional discussion of documenting compliance with quality control policies and procedures and paras. 5.08 through 5.11 for additional discussion of policies and procedures on independence, legal, and ethical requirements.

> d. document the auditor's understanding with an audited entity for which the auditor will provide a nonaudit service as indicated in paragraph 3.77; and
>
> e. document the evaluation of the significance of the threats created by providing any of the services discussed in paragraph 3.89.

Application Guidance: Documentation

3.108 Documentation of independence considerations provides evidence of the auditor's judgments in forming conclusions regarding compliance with independence requirements.

Professional Judgment

> **Requirement: Professional Judgment**
>
> **3.109** Auditors must use professional judgment in planning and conducting the engagement and in reporting the results.

Application Guidance: Professional Judgment

3.110 Professional judgment includes exercising reasonable care and professional skepticism. Reasonable care includes acting diligently in accordance with applicable professional standards and ethical principles. Attributes of professional skepticism include a questioning mind, awareness of conditions that may indicate possible misstatement owing to error or fraud, and a critical assessment of evidence. Professional skepticism includes being alert to, for example, evidence that contradicts other evidence obtained or information that brings into question the reliability of documents or responses to inquiries to be used as evidence. Further, it includes a mindset in which auditors assume that management is neither dishonest nor of unquestioned honesty. Auditors may accept records and documents as genuine unless they have reason to believe the contrary. Auditors may consider documenting procedures undertaken to support their application of professional skepticism in highly judgmental or subjective areas under audit.

3.111 Using the auditor's professional knowledge, skills, and abilities, in good faith and with integrity, to diligently gather information and objectively evaluate the sufficiency and appropriateness of evidence is a critical component of GAGAS engagements. Professional judgment and competence are interrelated because judgments made depend upon the auditor's competence, as discussed in chapter 4.

3.112 Professional judgment represents the application of the collective knowledge, skills, and abilities of all the personnel involved with an engagement, as well as the professional judgment of individual auditors. In addition, professional judgment may involve consultation with other stakeholders, specialists, and management in the audit organization.

3.113 Using professional judgment is important to auditors in carrying out all aspects of their professional responsibilities, including following the independence standards and related conceptual framework; maintaining objectivity and credibility; assigning competent personnel to the engagement; defining the scope of work; evaluating, documenting, and reporting the results of the work; and maintaining appropriate quality control over the engagement process.

3.114 Using professional judgment is important to auditors in applying the conceptual framework to determine independence in a given situation. This includes identifying and evaluating any threats to independence, including threats to the appearance of independence, and related safeguards that may mitigate the identified threats.[26]

3.115 Using professional judgment is important to auditors in determining the necessary level of understanding of the engagement subject matter and related circumstances. This includes considering whether the audit team's collective experience, training, knowledge, skills, abilities, and overall understanding are sufficient to assess the risks that the subject matter of the engagement may contain a significant inaccuracy or could be misinterpreted.[27]

3.116 An auditor's consideration of the risk level of each engagement, including the risk of arriving at improper conclusions, is also important. Within the context of audit risk, exercising professional judgment in determining the sufficiency and appropriateness of evidence to be used to support the findings and conclusions based on the engagement

---

[26]See para. 3.21b for a description of independence in appearance.

[27]See paras. 4.02 through 4.15 for a discussion of competence.

Chapter 3: Ethics, Independence, and
Professional Judgment

objectives and any recommendations reported is integral to the engagement process.

3.117 While this requirement places responsibility on each auditor and audit organization to exercise professional judgment in planning and conducting an engagement, it does not imply unlimited responsibility nor does it imply infallibility on the part of either the individual auditor or the audit organization. Absolute assurance is not attainable because of factors such as the nature of evidence and characteristics of fraud. Professional judgment does not mean eliminating all possible limitations or weaknesses associated with a specific engagement, but rather identifying, assessing, mitigating, and concluding on them.

Chapter 3: Ethics, Independence, and
Professional Judgment

Figure 1: Generally Accepted Government Auditing Standards Conceptual Framework for Independence

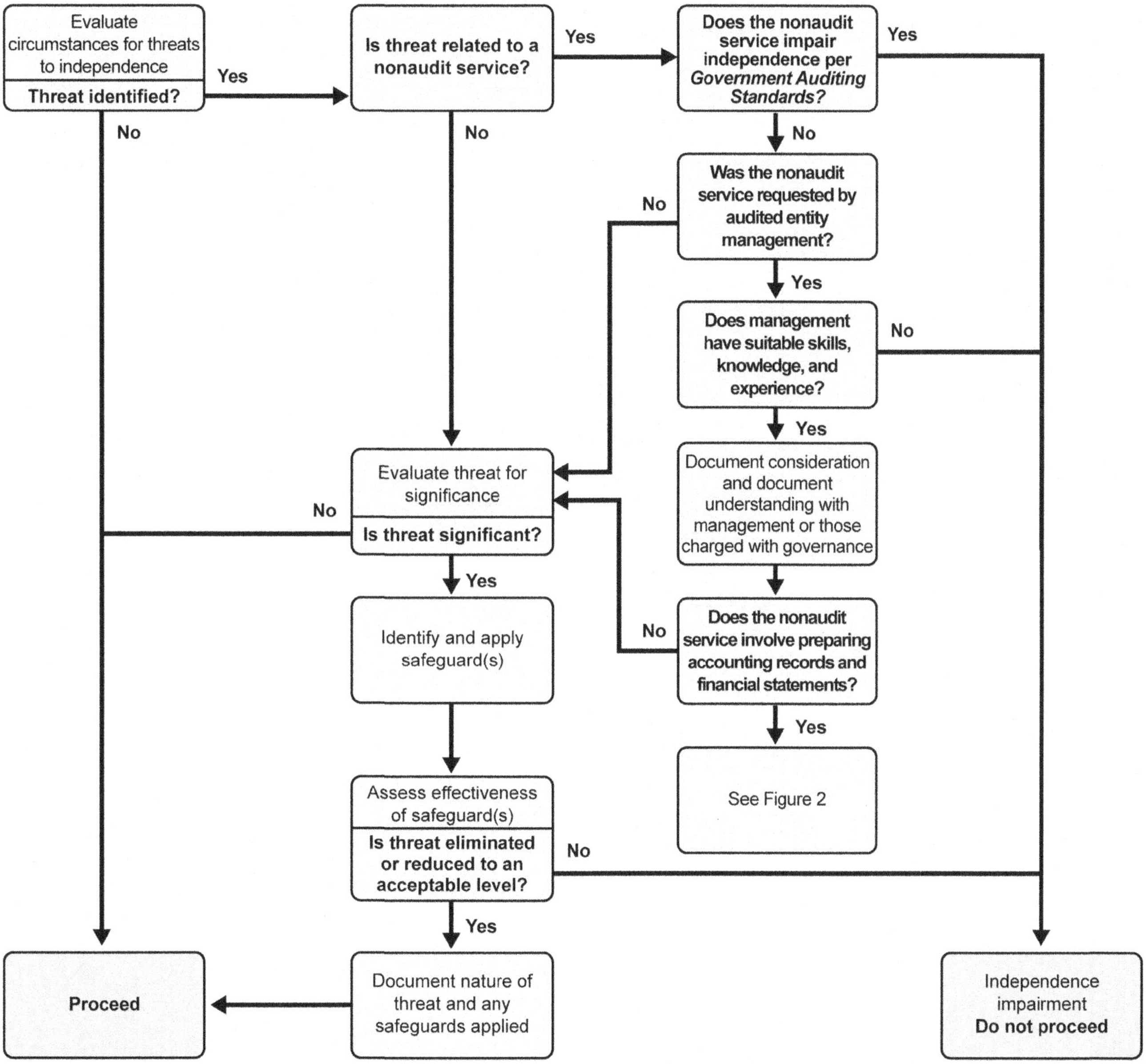

- Evaluate circumstances for threats to independence — **Threat identified?**
  - No → Proceed
  - Yes → Is threat related to a nonaudit service?
    - No → Evaluate threat for significance — **Is threat significant?**
    - Yes → Does the nonaudit service impair independence per *Government Auditing Standards*?
      - Yes → Independence impairment — **Do not proceed**
      - No → Was the nonaudit service requested by audited entity management?
        - No → Evaluate threat for significance — **Is threat significant?**
        - Yes → Does management have suitable skills, knowledge, and experience?
          - No → Independence impairment — **Do not proceed**
          - Yes → Document consideration and document understanding with management or those charged with governance → Does the nonaudit service involve preparing accounting records and financial statements?
            - No → Evaluate threat for significance
            - Yes → See Figure 2

- Evaluate threat for significance — **Is threat significant?**
  - No → Proceed
  - Yes → Identify and apply safeguard(s) → Assess effectiveness of safeguard(s) — **Is threat eliminated or reduced to an acceptable level?**
    - No → Independence impairment — **Do not proceed**
    - Yes → Document nature of threat and any safeguards applied → Proceed

Source: GAO. | GAO-18-568G

Chapter 3: Ethics, Independence, and Professional Judgment

Figure 2: Independence Considerations for Preparing Accounting Records and Financial Statements

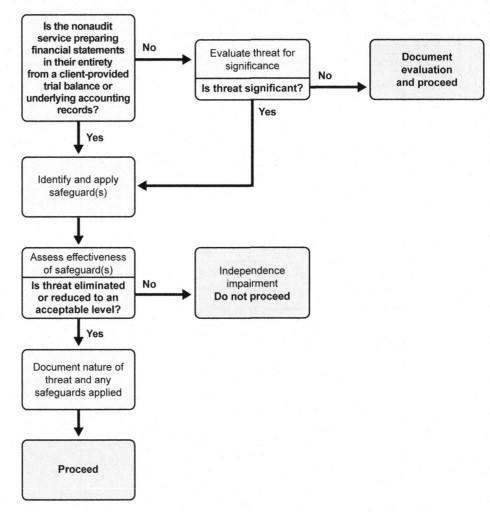

Source: GAO. | GAO-18-568G

Chapter 4: Competence and Continuing Professional Education

4.01 This chapter establishes the generally accepted government auditing standards (GAGAS) requirements for competence and continuing professional education (CPE). Competence includes being knowledgeable about the specific GAGAS requirements and having the skills and abilities to proficiently apply that knowledge on GAGAS engagements. CPE contributes to auditors' competence. The requirements of this chapter are intended to be followed in conjunction with all other applicable GAGAS requirements.

Competence

Requirements: General

4.02 The audit organization's management must assign auditors to conduct the engagement who before beginning work on the engagement collectively possess the competence needed to address the engagement objectives and perform their work in accordance with GAGAS.

4.03 The audit organization's management must assign auditors who before beginning work on the engagement possess the competence needed for their assigned roles.

4.04 The audit organization should have a process for recruitment, hiring, continuous development, assignment, and evaluation of personnel so that the workforce has the essential knowledge, skills, and abilities necessary to conduct the engagement. The nature, extent, and formality of the process will depend on various factors, such as the size of the audit organization, its structure, and its work.

Application Guidance: General

4.05 Competence is the knowledge, skills, and abilities, obtained from education and experience, necessary to conduct the GAGAS engagement. Competence enables auditors to make sound professional judgments. Competence includes possessing the technical knowledge and skills necessary for the assigned role and the type of work being done. This includes possessing specific knowledge about GAGAS.

4.06 Competence is derived from a combination of education and experience. Education is a structured and systematic process aimed at developing knowledge, skills, and other abilities; it is a process that is typically but not exclusively conducted in academic or learning environments. Experience refers to workplace activities that are relevant to developing professional proficiency. Competence is not necessarily measured by years of auditing experience because such a quantitative measurement may not accurately reflect the kinds of experiences gained by auditors in any given time period. Maintaining competence through a commitment to learning and development throughout auditors' professional lives is an important element for auditors.

Application Guidance: Indicators of Competence

Technical Knowledge and Skills

4.07 The knowledge, skills, and abilities needed when conducting an engagement in accordance with GAGAS include the understanding necessary to proficiently apply

    a. GAGAS;

    b. standards, statutory requirements, regulations, criteria, and guidance applicable to auditing or the objectives for the engagement(s) being conducted; and

    c. techniques, tools, and guidance related to professional expertise applicable to the work being performed.

Auditor proficiency in these areas helps ensure that engagements are conducted in accordance with GAGAS.

4.08 Achieving the knowledge, skills, and abilities needed to conduct a GAGAS engagement may include

    a. having prior experience in the subject matter or type of engagement;

    b. completing CPE related to the subject matter or type of engagement; and

    c. obtaining degrees or certifications relevant to the subject matter or type of engagement.

Competence for Assigned Roles

4.09 The audit organization and engagement teams may consider the levels of proficiency needed for each role on the engagement when assigning auditors to the engagement.

4.10 Roles on the engagement generally include the following:

a. Nonsupervisory auditors: Auditors in these roles plan or perform engagement procedures. Work situations for these auditors are characterized by low levels of ambiguity, complexity, and uncertainty. The nonsupervisory auditor role necessitates at least a basic level of proficiency.

b. Supervisory auditors: Auditors in these roles plan engagements, perform engagement procedures, or direct engagements. Work situations for these auditors are characterized by moderate levels of ambiguity, complexity, and uncertainty. The supervisory auditor role necessitates at least an intermediate level of proficiency.

c. Partners and directors: Auditors in these roles plan engagements, perform engagement procedures, or direct or report on engagements. Partners and directors may also be responsible for reviewing engagement quality prior to issuing the report, for signing the report, or both. Work situations for these auditors are characterized by high levels of ambiguity, complexity, and uncertainty. The partner and director role necessitates an advanced level of proficiency.

4.11 Definitions of key terms follow:

a. Planning: Determining engagement objectives, scope, and methodology; establishing criteria to evaluate matters subject to audit; or coordinating the work of the other audit organizations. This definition excludes auditors whose role is limited to gathering information used in planning the engagement.

b. Directing: Supervising the efforts of others who are involved in accomplishing the objectives of the engagement or reviewing engagement work to determine whether those objectives have been accomplished.

c. Performing engagement procedures: Performing tests and procedures necessary to accomplish the engagement objectives in accordance with GAGAS.

d. Reporting: Determining the report content and substance or reviewing reports to determine whether the engagement objectives have been accomplished and the evidence supports the report's technical content and substance prior to issuance. This includes signing the report.

Requirement: Specialists

4.12 The engagement team should determine that specialists assisting the engagement team on a GAGAS engagement are qualified and competent in their areas of specialization.

Application Guidance: Specialists

4.13 Some engagements may necessitate the use of specialized techniques or methods that call for the skills of specialists. Specialists do not include individuals with special skill or knowledge related to specialized areas within the field of accounting or auditing, such as income taxation and information technology. Such individuals are considered auditors.

4.14 The competence and qualifications of specialists significantly affect whether their work will be adequate for the engagement team's purposes and will meet GAGAS requirements. Competence of specialists relates to the nature and level of expertise. Qualifications of specialists relate to their professional certifications, reputations, and previous work in the subject matter. Other relevant factors include the ability of specialists to exercise competence in the circumstances of the engagement and the effects that bias, conflict of interest, or the influence of others may have on the specialists' professional judgment.

4.15 Sources that may inform the auditors' assessment of the competence and professional qualifications of a specialist include the following:

a. the professional certification, license, or other recognition of the competence of the specialist in his or her field, as appropriate;

b. the reputation and standing of the specialist in the views of peers and others familiar with the specialist's capability or performance;

c. the specialist's experience and previous work in the subject matter;

d. the auditors' assessment of the specialist's knowledge and qualification based on prior experience in using the specialist's work;

e. the specialist's knowledge of any technical performance standards or other professional or industry requirements in the specialist's field (for example, ethical standards and other membership requirements of a professional body or industry association, accreditation standards of a licensing body, or requirements imposed by law or regulation);

f. the knowledge of the specialist with respect to relevant auditing standards; and

g. the assessment of unexpected events, changes in conditions, or the evidence obtained from the results of engagement procedures that indicate it may be necessary to reconsider the initial evaluation of the competence and qualifications of a specialist as the engagement progresses.

Continuing Professional Education

Requirements: General

4.16 Auditors who plan, direct, perform engagement procedures for, or report on an engagement conducted in accordance with GAGAS should develop and maintain their professional competence by completing at least 80 hours of CPE in every 2-year period as follows.

CPE hours	Subject matter categories of CPE
24 hours	Subject matter directly related to the government environment, government auditing, or the specific or unique environment in which the audited entity operates
56 hours	Subject matter that directly enhance auditors' professional expertise to conduct engagements

4.17 Auditors should complete at least 20 hours of CPE in each year of the 2-year periods.

4.18 The audit organization should maintain documentation of each auditor's CPE.[28]

Application Guidance: General

4.19 The continuing competence of the audit organization's personnel depends, in part, on an appropriate level of CPE so that auditors maintain the knowledge, skills, and abilities necessary to conduct the GAGAS engagement. Obtaining CPE specifically on GAGAS, particularly during years in which there are revisions to the standards, may assist auditors in maintaining the competence necessary to conduct GAGAS engagements.

4.20 CPE used to fulfill the 24-hour requirement may be taken at any time during the 2-year measurement period.

Application Guidance: Subject Matter Categories of CPE

4.21 Determining what subjects are appropriate for individual auditors to satisfy the CPE requirements is a matter of professional judgment to be exercised by auditors in consultation with appropriate officials in their audit organization. When determining what specific subjects qualify for the CPE requirement, the auditors may consider the types of knowledge, skills, and abilities, and the level of proficiency necessary, in order to be competent for their assigned roles. Auditors may consider probable future engagements to which they may be assigned when selecting specific CPE subjects to satisfy the 24-hour and the 56-hour CPE requirements. The audit organization is ultimately responsible for determining whether a subject or topic qualifies as acceptable for its auditors.

4.22 The subject matter categories for the 24-hour requirement may be used to satisfy the 56-hour CPE requirement. If CPE in any of the subject matter and topics that would satisfy the 56-hour requirement, as discussed in paragraph 4.24, is tailored specifically to the government environment, such CPE may qualify toward satisfying the 24-hour

---

[28]See paras. 4.51 and 5.16 for a discussion of CPE documentation.

Chapter 4: Competence and Continuing
Professional Education

requirement. Examples of CPE subjects that may qualify for each of the categories are listed below.

Subject Matter Directly Related to the Government Environment, Government Auditing, or the Specific or Unique Environment in Which the Audited Entity Operates (24-Hour Requirement)

4.23 Subject matter directly related to the government environment, government auditing, or the specific or unique environment in which the audited entity operates may include, but is not limited to, the following:

   a. generally accepted government auditing standards (GAGAS) and related topics, such as internal control as addressed in GAGAS;

   b. the applicable American Institute of Certified Public Accountants' (AICPA) Statements on Auditing Standards;[29]

   c. the applicable AICPA Statements on Standards for Attestation Engagements and Statements on Standards for Accounting and Review Services;[30]

   d. the applicable auditing standards issued by the Institute of Internal Auditors, the Public Company Accounting and Oversight Board, the International Auditing and Assurance Standards Board, or other auditing standard-setting body;

   e. U.S. generally accepted accounting principles, or the applicable financial reporting framework being used, such as those issued by the Federal Accounting Standards Advisory Board, the Governmental Accounting Standards Board, or the Financial Accounting Standards Board;

   f. *Standards for Internal Control in the Federal Government*;[31]

---

[29]See para. 6.01 for a discussion of the AICPA standards incorporated into GAGAS for financial audits.

[30]See para. 7.01 for a discussion of the AICPA standards incorporated into GAGAS for attestation engagements and reviews of financial statements.

[31]GAO, *Standards for Internal Control in the Federal Government*, GAO-14-704G (Washington, D.C.: September 2014).

g. *Internal Control—Integrated Framework*,[32] as applicable;

h. requirements for recipients of federal contracts or grants, such as Single Audits under the *Uniform Administrative Requirements, Cost Principles, and Audit Requirements for Federal Awards*;[33]

i. requirements for federal, state, or local program audits;

j. relevant or applicable audit standards or guides, including those for information technology auditing and forensic auditing;

k. information technology auditing topics applicable to the government environment;

l. fraud topics applicable to a government environment;

m. statutory requirements, regulations, criteria, guidance, trends, risks, or topics relevant to the specific and unique environment in which the audited entity operates;

n. statutory requirements, regulations, criteria, guidance, trends, risks, or topics relevant to the subject matter of the engagement, such as scientific, medical, environmental, educational, or any other specialized subject matter;

o. topics directly related to the government environment, such as the nature of government (structures, financing, and operations), economic or other conditions and pressures facing governments, common government financial management issues, appropriations, measurement or evaluation of government financial or program performance, and application of general audit methodologies or techniques to a government environment or program;

---

[32]Committee of Sponsoring Organizations of the Treadway Commission, *Internal Control—Integrated Framework* (New York: American Institute of Certified Public Accountants, 2013).

[33]See Part 200, Subpart F, of Title 2, *Code of Federal Regulations*.

Chapter 4: Competence and Continuing Professional Education

p. specialized audit methodologies or analytical techniques, such as the use of complex survey instruments, actuarial estimates, statistical analysis tests, or statistical or nonstatistical sampling;

q. performance auditing topics, such as obtaining evidence, professional skepticism, and other applicable audit skills;[34]

r. government ethics and independence;

s. partnerships between governments, businesses, and citizens;

t. legislative policies and procedures;

u. topics related to fraud, waste, abuse, or improper payments affecting government entities; and

v. compliance with laws and regulations.

Subject Matter That Directly Enhances Auditors' Professional Expertise to Conduct Engagements (56-Hour Requirement)

4.24 Subject matter that directly enhances auditors' professional expertise to conduct engagements may include, but is not limited to, the following:

a. subject matter categories for the 24-hour requirement listed in paragraph 4.23;

b. general ethics and independence;

c. topics related to accounting, acquisitions management, asset management, budgeting, cash management, contracting, data analysis, program performance, or procurement;

d. communicating clearly and effectively, both orally and in writing;

e. managing time and resources;

f. leadership;

---

[34] See chs. 8 and 9 for performance audit topics that may be included.

g. software applications used in conducting engagements;

h. information technology; and

i. economics, human capital management, social and political sciences, and other academic disciplines that may be applied in engagements, as applicable.

Application Guidance: Exemptions and Exceptions

4.25 Auditors may be exempted from the 56-hour CPE requirement by the audit organization, but not the 24-hour requirement, if they

a. charge less than 20 percent of their time annually to engagements conducted in accordance with GAGAS and

b. are only involved in performing engagement procedures, but not involved in planning, directing, or reporting on the engagement.

The 20 percent may be based on historical or estimated charges in a year, provided that the audit organization has a basis for this determination and monitors actual time. For auditors who change status such that they are charging more than 20 percent of their time annually to engagements under GAGAS, the audit organization may prorate the required CPE hours similar to when auditors are assigned to GAGAS engagements after the beginning of a 2-year CPE measurement period, as discussed in paragraph 4.42.

4.26 Nonsupervisory auditors who charge less than 40 hours of their time annually to engagements conducted in accordance with GAGAS may be exempted by the organization from all CPE requirements in paragraph 4.16.

4.27 The audit organization may exempt from the CPE requirements college and university students employed on a temporary basis for a limited period of time (for example, an internship of limited duration) or enrolled in a formal program sponsored by the college or university for a specific period of employment, such as a term or semester.

4.28 Employees or contract employees performing support services within the audit organization, such as individuals who are assigned to positions in budgeting, human resources, training, and administrative functions, and who do not conduct engagement activities are not auditors subject to the GAGAS CPE requirements. Employees or contract employees who assist in the engagement by performing support services, such as performing background research, data entry, writing and editing assistance, proofreading, or report production and distribution are not auditors subject to the GAGAS CPE requirements.

4.29 The audit organization, at its discretion, may grant exemptions from a portion of the CPE requirement in the event of extended absences or other extenuating circumstances if situations such as the following prevent auditors from fulfilling those requirements and conducting engagements:

a. ill health,

b. maternity or paternity leave,

c. extended family leave,

d. sabbaticals,

e. leave without pay absences,

f. foreign residency,

g. military service, and

h. disasters.

The audit organization may not grant exceptions for reasons such as workload, budget, or travel constraints.

Application Guidance: Specialists

4.30 External specialists are not auditors subject to the GAGAS CPE requirements. Also, internal specialists assisting on a GAGAS engagement who are not involved in planning, directing, performing engagement procedures, or reporting on a GAGAS engagement are not auditors subject to the GAGAS CPE requirements.

4.31 Internal specialists who are performing work in accordance with GAGAS as part of the engagement team—including planning, directing, performing engagement procedures, or reporting on a GAGAS engagement—are considered auditors and are subject to the GAGAS

CPE requirements. The GAGAS CPE requirements become effective for internal specialists when an audit organization first assigns an internal specialist to an engagement. Because internal specialists apply specialized knowledge in government engagements, CPE in their areas of specialization qualifies under the requirement for 24 hours of CPE that directly relates to government auditing, the government environment, or the specific or unique environment in which the audited entity operates.

Application Guidance: Programs and Activities That Qualify for CPE

4.32 CPE programs are structured educational activities or programs with learning objectives designed to maintain or enhance the auditors' competence to address engagement objectives and perform work in accordance with GAGAS.

4.33 The following are examples of structured educational programs and activities:

a. internal training programs (e.g., courses, seminars, and workshops);

b. education and development programs presented at conferences, conventions, meetings, and seminars and meetings or workshops of professional organizations;

c. training programs presented by other audit organizations, educational organizations, foundations, and associations;

d. web-based seminars and individual-study or eLearning programs;

e. audio conferences;

f. accredited university and college courses (credit and noncredit);

g. standard-setting organization, professional organization, or audit organization staff meetings when a structured educational program with learning objectives is presented (e.g., the portion of the meeting that is a structured educational program with learning objectives designed to maintain or enhance auditors' competence);

h. correspondence courses, individual-study guides, and workbooks;

i. serving as a speaker, panelist, instructor, or discussion leader at programs that qualify for CPE hours;

j. developing or technical review of courses or the course materials for programs that qualify for CPE hours; and

k. publishing articles and books that contribute directly to the author's professional proficiency to conduct engagements.

4.34 Individual auditors who are members of professional organizations or who are licensed professionals, such as certified public accountants, are cautioned that the GAGAS CPE requirements, while similar in many respects to those of professional organizations and of licensing bodies, may not be identical. Some subjects and topics may be acceptable to state licensing bodies or professional organizations, but may not qualify as CPE under GAGAS. Conversely, some CPE that qualifies for GAGAS may not qualify for state licensing bodies or professional organizations. Careful consideration of auditors' relevant professional organizations or licensing body requirements is encouraged to meet other relevant CPE requirements.

4.35 Examples of training topics that may qualify as CPE for state licensing bodies or professional organizations but would not generally qualify as CPE for purposes of satisfying requirements under GAGAS include certain training in taxation, personal financial planning and investment, taxation strategies, estate planning, retirement planning, and practice management, unless such training directly enhances the auditors' professional proficiency to perform engagements or relate to the subject matter of an engagement. However, if certain taxation or other topics relate to an objective or the subject matter of an engagement, training in those related topics could qualify as CPE under GAGAS.

4.36 Examples of programs and activities that do not qualify for CPE hours under GAGAS include, but are not limited to, the following:

a. on-the-job training;

b. basic or elementary courses in subjects or topics in which auditors already have the knowledge and skills being taught;

c. programs that are designed for general personal development, such as résumé writing, improving parent-child relations, personal investments and money management, and retirement planning;

d. programs that demonstrate office equipment or software that is not used in conducting engagements;

e. programs that provide training on the audit organization's administrative operations;

f. business sessions at professional organization conferences, conventions, and meetings that do not have a structured educational program with learning objectives;

g. conducting external quality control reviews; and

h. sitting for professional certification examinations.

Basic or elementary courses would be acceptable in cases where they are deemed necessary as "refresher" courses to enhance the auditors' proficiency to conduct audits and attestation engagements.

Application Guidance: Measurement of CPE

4.37 A CPE hour may be granted for each 50 minutes of participation in programs and activities that qualify.

4.38 For university or college credit courses, each unit of college credit under a semester system equals 15 CPE hours, and each unit of college credit under a quarter system equals 10 CPE hours. For university or college noncredit courses, CPE hours may be granted only for the actual classroom time.

4.39 For individual-study programs where successful completion is measured by a summary examination, CPE credit may be granted if auditors complete the examination with a passing grade. Auditors in other individual-study programs may earn CPE hours when they satisfactorily complete the requirements of the self-study program. The number of hours granted may be based on the CPE provider's recommended number of CPE hours for the program.

4.40 Speakers, instructors, and discussion leaders at programs that qualify for CPE and auditors who develop or write the course materials may receive CPE hours for preparation and presentation time to the extent the subject matter contributes to auditors' competence. One CPE hour may be granted for each 50 minutes of presentation time. Up to 2 CPE hours may be granted for developing, writing, or advance preparation for each 50 minutes of the presentation. Auditors may not receive CPE hours for either preparation or presentation time for repeated presentations that they make within the 2-year period, unless the subject matter involved was changed significantly for each presentation. The maximum number of CPE hours that may be granted to an auditor as a speaker, instructor, discussion leader, or preparer of course materials may not exceed 40 hours for any 2-year period.

4.41 Articles, books, or materials written by auditors and published on subjects and topics that contribute directly to professional proficiency to conduct engagements qualify for CPE hours in the year they are published. One CPE hour may be granted for each hour devoted to writing articles, books, or materials that are published. However, CPE hours for published writings may not exceed 20 hours for any 2-year period.

4.42 Auditors hired or assigned to a GAGAS engagement after the beginning of an audit organization's 2-year CPE period may complete a prorated number of CPE hours. An audit organization may define a prorated number of hours based on the number of full 6-month intervals remaining in the CPE period. For example, an audit organization has a 2-year CPE period running from January 1, 2020, through December 31, 2021. The audit organization assigns a new auditor to a GAGAS engagement in May 2020. The audit organization may calculate the prorated CPE requirement for the auditor as follows:

   a. Number of full 6-month intervals remaining in the CPE period: 3

   b. Number of 6-month intervals in the full 2-year period: 4

   c. Newly assigned auditor's CPE requirement: 3/4 x 80 hours = 60 hours

When auditors are newly hired or newly assigned to GAGAS engagements and have had some previous CPE, the audit organization has flexibility and may choose between using a pro rata approach or evaluating whether and to what extent any CPE already taken in that period would satisfy GAGAS CPE requirements.

4.43 For newly assigned auditors who are subject to the 24-hour requirement, the number of prorated hours may be calculated in a similar manner: 3/4 x 24 hours = 18 hours, in this example. The prorated amount of hours would be the total requirement over the partial period. The 20-

Chapter 4: Competence and Continuing Professional Education

hour minimum for each CPE year would not apply when the prorated number of hours is being used to cover a partial 2-year CPE period.

4.44 At their discretion, audit organizations may give auditors who have not completed the 80-hour CPE requirement for any 2-year period up to 2 months immediately following the 2-year period to make up the deficiency. Audit organizations may also give auditors who have not completed the 20 hours of CPE in a 1-year period up to 2 months immediately following the 1-year period to make up the deficiency. Any CPE hours completed toward a deficiency in one period may be documented in the CPE records and may not be counted toward the requirements for the next period. Audit organizations that grant the 2-month grace period may not allow auditors who have not satisfied the CPE requirements after the grace period to participate in GAGAS engagements until those requirements are satisfied.

4.45 Auditors may not carry over CPE hours earned in excess of the 80-hour and 24-hour requirements from one 2-year CPE measurement period to the next.

4.46 If an audit organization discontinues conducting GAGAS engagements or reassigns auditors to non-GAGAS assignments before auditors complete the CPE requirements, the auditors are not required to complete the number of hours to satisfy the CPE requirements. However, the audit organization may wish to have its auditors complete those requirements if it is foreseeable that the auditors will conduct GAGAS engagements in the future.

4.47 Auditors who complete a professional certification review course may receive CPE hours only for those segments of the review course that are relevant to the standards, statutory requirements, regulations, criteria, and guidance applicable to auditing or to the engagement objectives being performed, or for subject matter that directly enhances auditors' professional expertise to conduct engagements.

4.48 To simplify administration of the CPE requirements, an audit organization may establish a standard 2-year period for all of its auditors, which can be on either a fixed-year or rolling-year basis. A fixed-year measurement period, for example, would be the 2-year periods 2019 through 2020, 2021 through 2022, and so forth, while a rolling-year measurement period would be 2019 through 2020, 2020 through 2021, 2021 through 2022, and so forth.

4.49 An audit organization may use a measurement date other than the date it started its first GAGAS engagement, or the audit organization may choose to change its measurement date to coincide with a fiscal year or another reporting requirement, such as one established by a state licensing body or professional organization. For example, if an audit organization changes the end date of the measurement period from December 31 to June 30, during the audit organization's transition period (January 1 to June 30), its auditors may complete at least a prorated number of CPE hours for the 6-month transition period. The number of prorated hours required may be calculated using the method illustrated in paragraphs 4.42 and 4.43.

Application Guidance: Monitoring CPE

4.50 The audit organization's policies and procedures for CPE may address the following:

a. identifying all auditors required to meet the CPE requirements;

b. providing auditors with the opportunity to attend internal CPE programs, external CPE programs, or both;

c. assisting auditors in determining which programs, activities, and subjects qualify for CPE;

d. documenting the number of CPE hours completed by each auditor; and

e. monitoring auditor compliance with the CPE requirements to ensure that auditors complete sufficient CPE in qualifying programs and subjects.

4.51 Policies and procedures for documentation may address maintaining documentation of the CPE hours completed by each auditor subject to the CPE requirements for an appropriate period of time to satisfy any legal and administrative requirements, including peer review. The audit organization may maintain documentation of CPE or may delegate the responsibility to the auditor and put in place adequate procedures to ensure that its records of CPE hours earned by auditors are supported by the documentation maintained by auditors. Documentation may include the following information:

a. the name of the organization providing the CPE;

b. the title of the training program, including the subject matter or field of study;

c. the dates attended for group programs or dates completed for individual study programs;

d. the number of CPE hours earned toward the 56-hour and 24-hour requirements;

e. any reasons for specific exceptions granted to the CPE requirement; and

f. evidence of completion of CPE, such as a certificate or other evidence of completion from the CPE provider for group and individual-study programs, if provided; documentation of CPE courses presented or copies of course materials developed by or for speakers, instructors, or discussion leaders, along with a written statement supporting the number of CPE hours claimed; or a copy of the published book, article, or other material that name the writer as author or contributor, or a written statement from the writer supporting the number of CPE hours claimed.

4.52 The audit organization may monitor CPE compliance through its internal inspections or other quality assurance monitoring activities.

4.53 The audit organization is not required to prepare reports on CPE. However, the audit organization may consider preparing a periodic CPE report for distribution to the auditors or maintaining or accessing training data online to monitor its auditors' progress toward meeting the CPE requirements.

Chapter 5: Quality Control and Peer Review

5.01 This chapter establishes the generally accepted government auditing standards (GAGAS) requirements and guidance for quality control and assurance, and for administering, planning, performing, and reporting on peer reviews of audit organizations that conduct engagements in accordance with GAGAS. The requirements of this chapter are intended to be followed in conjunction with those of all other applicable GAGAS requirements.

Quality Control and Assurance

Requirement: Quality Control and Assurance

5.02 An audit organization conducting engagements in accordance with GAGAS must establish and maintain a system of quality control that is designed to provide the audit organization with reasonable assurance that the organization and its personnel comply with professional standards and applicable legal and regulatory requirements.

Application Guidance: Quality Control and Assurance

5.03 An audit organization's system of quality control encompasses the organization's leadership, emphasis on performing high-quality work, and policies and procedures designed to provide reasonable assurance of complying with professional standards and applicable legal and regulatory requirements. The nature, extent, and formality of an audit organization's quality control system will vary based on the audit organization's circumstances, such as size, number of offices and geographic dispersion, knowledge and experience of its personnel, nature and complexity of its engagement work, and cost-benefit considerations.

System of Quality Control

Requirement: System of Quality Control

5.04 An audit organization should document its quality control policies and procedures and communicate those policies and procedures to its personnel. The audit organization should document compliance with its quality control policies and procedures and maintain such documentation for a period of time sufficient to enable those performing monitoring procedures and peer reviews to evaluate the extent to which the audit organization complies with its quality control policies and procedures.

Leadership Responsibilities for Quality within the Audit Organization

Requirements: Leadership Responsibilities for Quality within the Audit Organization

5.05 The audit organization should establish policies and procedures on leadership responsibilities for quality within the audit organization that include designating responsibility for quality of engagements conducted in accordance with GAGAS and communicating policies and procedures relating to quality.

5.06 The audit organization should establish policies and procedures designed to provide reasonable assurance that those assigned operational responsibility for the audit organization's system of quality control have sufficient and appropriate experience and ability, and the necessary authority, to assume that responsibility.

Application Guidance: Leadership Responsibilities for Quality within the Audit Organization

5.07 Appropriate policies and communications encourage a culture that recognizes that quality is essential in conducting GAGAS engagements and that audit organization leadership is ultimately responsible for the system of quality control.

Independence, Legal, and Ethical Requirements

Requirements: Independence, Legal, and Ethical Requirements

5.08 The audit organization should establish policies and procedures on independence and legal and ethical requirements that are designed to provide reasonable assurance that the organization and its

> personnel maintain independence and comply with applicable legal and ethical requirements.[35]
>
> **5.09** At least annually, the audit organization should obtain written affirmation of compliance with its policies and procedures on independence from all of its personnel required to be independent.

Application Guidance: Independence, Legal, and Ethical Requirements

5.10 Policies and procedures pertaining to independence and legal and ethical requirements assist the audit organization in

   a. communicating its independence requirements to its personnel and

   b. identifying and evaluating circumstances and relationships that create threats to independence and taking appropriate action to eliminate those threats or reduce them to an acceptable level by applying safeguards or, if considered appropriate, withdrawing from the engagement where withdrawal is not prohibited by law or regulation.

5.11 Written affirmation of compliance with its policies and procedures on independence from all audit organization personnel required to be independent may be in paper or electronic form. By obtaining affirmation of retrospective compliance with the audit organization's policies and procedures on independence during a specified period and taking appropriate action on information indicating noncompliance, or potential noncompliance, the organization demonstrates the importance that it attaches to independence and keeps the issue current for, and visible to, its personnel. An audit organization may obtain affirmation of required personnel's compliance with policies and procedures on independence more frequently than once per year. For example, affirmation may be obtained on a per-engagement basis when such engagements last less than 1 year.

---

[35]See paras. 3.02 through 3.16 for a discussion of ethical principles and paras. 3.18 through 3.108 for independence requirements and guidance.

Chapter 5: Quality Control and Peer Review

Initiation, Acceptance, and Continuance of Engagements

Requirement: Initiation, Acceptance, and Continuance of Engagements

5.12 The audit organization should establish policies and procedures for the initiation, acceptance, and continuance of engagements that are designed to provide reasonable assurance that the organization will undertake engagements only if it

a. complies with professional standards, applicable legal and regulatory requirements, and ethical principles;

b. acts within its legal mandate or authority; and

c. has the capabilities, including time and resources, to do so.

Application Guidance: Initiation, Acceptance, and Continuance of Engagements

5.13 Government audit organizations initiate engagements as a result of (1) legal mandates, (2) requests from legislative bodies or oversight bodies, and (3) audit organization discretion. In the case of legal mandates and requests, a government audit organization may be required to conduct the engagement and may not be permitted to make decisions about acceptance or continuance and may not be permitted to resign or withdraw from the engagement.

5.14 Audit organizations may operate with limited resources. Audit organizations may consider their workloads in determining whether they have the resources to deliver the range of work to the desired level of quality. To achieve this, audit organizations may develop systems to prioritize their work in a way that takes into account the need to maintain quality.

Human Resources

Requirements: Human Resources

5.15 The audit organization should establish policies and procedures for human resources that are designed to provide the organization with reasonable assurance that it has personnel with the competence to conduct GAGAS engagements in accordance with professional standards and applicable legal and regulatory requirements.[36]

5.16 The audit organization should establish policies and procedures to provide reasonable assurance that auditors who are performing work in accordance with GAGAS meet the continuing professional education (CPE) requirements, including maintaining documentation of the CPE completed and any exemptions granted.

Application Guidance: Human Resources

5.17 Effective recruitment processes and procedures help the audit organization select individuals of integrity who have the capacity to develop the competence and capabilities necessary to perform the audit organization's work and possess the appropriate characteristics to enable them to perform competently. Examples of such characteristics include meeting minimum academic requirements established by the audit organization and leadership traits.

5.18 The audit organization may use a suitably qualified external person to conduct engagement work when internal resources, for example, personnel with particular areas of technical expertise, are unavailable.

5.19 Effective performance evaluation, compensation, and advancement procedures give due recognition and reward to developing and maintaining competent personnel. Steps that an audit organization may take in developing and maintaining competent personnel include the following:

a. making personnel aware of the audit organization's expectations regarding performance and ethical principles;

b. providing personnel with an evaluation of, and counseling on, performance, progress, and career development; and

c. helping personnel understand that compensation and advancement to positions of greater responsibility depend on, among other things, performance quality, and that failure to

---

[36]Refer to paras. 4.02 through 4.15 for requirements and guidance on competence.

comply with the audit organization's policies and procedures may result in disciplinary action.

5.20 The size and circumstances of the audit organization are important considerations in determining the structure of the audit organization's performance evaluation process. A smaller audit organization, in particular, may employ less formal methods of evaluating the performance of its personnel.

5.21 Objectives of the audit organization's human resources policies and procedures may include

a. promoting learning and training for all personnel to encourage their professional development and to help ensure that personnel are trained in current developments in the profession and

b. helping ensure that personnel and any parties contracted to carry out work for the audit organization have an appropriate understanding of the environment(s) in which the organization operates and a good understanding of the work they are required to carry out.

Engagement Performance

Requirements: General

5.22 The audit organization should establish policies and procedures for engagement performance, documentation, and reporting that are designed to provide the audit organization with reasonable assurance that engagements are conducted and reports are issued in accordance with professional standards and applicable legal and regulatory requirements.

5.23 If auditors change the engagement objectives during the engagement, they should document the revised engagement objectives and the reasons for the changes.

5.24 The audit organization should establish policies and procedures designed to provide it with reasonable assurance that

a. appropriate consultation takes place on difficult or contentious issues that arise among engagement team members in the course of conducting a GAGAS engagement;

b. both the individual seeking consultation and the individual consulted document and agree upon the nature and scope of such consultations; and

c. the conclusions resulting from consultations are documented, understood by both the individual seeking consultation and the individual consulted, and implemented.

5.25 If an engagement is terminated before it is completed and an audit report is not issued, auditors should document the results of the work to the date of termination and why the engagement was terminated.

Application Guidance: General

5.26 The audit organization's policies and procedures may address consistency in the quality of engagement performance. This is often accomplished through written or electronic manuals, software tools or other forms of standardized documentation, and industry-specific or subject matter-specific guidance materials. Matters addressed may include the following:

a. maintaining current policies and procedures;

b. briefing the engagement team to provide an understanding of the engagement objectives and professional standards;

c. complying with applicable engagement standards;

d. planning the engagement, supervision, staff training, and mentoring;

e. reviewing the work performed, the significant judgments made, and the type of report being issued;

f. documenting the work performed and the timing and extent of review;

g. reviewing the independence and qualifications of any specialists and the scope and quality of their work;

h. resolving difficult or contentious issues or disagreements among team members, including specialists;

i. obtaining and addressing comments from the audited entity on draft reports; and

j. reporting findings and conclusions supported by the evidence obtained and in accordance with professional standards and applicable legal and regulatory requirements.

5.27 The form and content of the documentation of the audit organization's policies and procedures, as well as documentation of its compliance with those policies and procedures, are matters of professional judgment and will vary based on the organization's circumstances.

5.28 Documentation of policies and procedures, as well as compliance with those policies and procedures, may be either electronic or manual. For example, large audit organizations may use electronic databases to document matters such as independence confirmations, performance evaluations, and the results of monitoring. Smaller audit organizations may use more informal methods in the documentation of their systems of quality control, such as manual notes, checklists, and forms.

5.29 Consultation includes discussion at the appropriate professional level with individuals within or outside the audit organization who have relevant specialized expertise.

5.30 Consultation uses appropriate research resources, as well as the collective experience and technical expertise of the audit organization. Consultation helps promote quality and improves the application of professional judgment. Appropriate recognition of consultation in the audit organization's policies and procedures helps promote a culture in which consultation is recognized as a strength and personnel are encouraged to consult on difficult or contentious issues.

5.31 Effective consultation on significant technical, ethical, and other matters within the audit organization or, when applicable, outside the audit organization can be achieved when

a. those consulted are given all the relevant facts that will enable them to provide informed advice;

b. those consulted have appropriate knowledge, authority, and experience; and

c. conclusions resulting from consultations are appropriately documented and implemented.

5.32 Documentation of consultations with other professionals that involve difficult or contentious matters contributes to an understanding of

a. the issue on which consultation was sought and

b. the results of the consultation, including any decisions made, the basis for those decisions, and how they were implemented.

5.33 An audit organization needing to obtain specialized or technical expertise from external providers may take advantage of services provided by

a. other audit organizations,

b. professional and regulatory bodies, and

c. commercial organizations that provide relevant quality control services.

5.34 Before contracting for services, consideration of the competence and capabilities of the external provider helps the audit organization determine whether the external provider is suitably qualified for that purpose.

5.35 Determining whether and how to communicate the reason for terminating an engagement or changing the engagement objectives to those charged with governance, appropriate officials of the audited entity, the entity contracting for or requesting the engagement, and other appropriate officials will depend on the facts and circumstances and therefore is a matter of professional judgment.

Requirements: Supervision

5.36 The audit organization should establish policies and procedures that require engagement team members with appropriate levels of skill and proficiency in auditing to supervise engagements and review work performed by other engagement team members.

5.37 The audit organization should assign responsibility for each engagement to an engagement partner or director with authority designated by the audit organization to assume that responsibility and should establish policies and procedures requiring the organization to

a. communicate the identity and role of the engagement partner or director to management and those charged with governance of the audited entity and

b. clearly define the responsibilities of the engagement partner or director and communicate them to that individual.

Application Guidance: Supervision

5.38 Appropriate teamwork and training help less experienced members of the engagement team to clearly understand the objectives of the assigned work.

5.39 Engagement supervision includes the following:

a. tracking the progress of the engagement;

b. considering the competence of individual members of the engagement team, whether they understand their instructions, and whether the work is being carried out in accordance with the planned approach to the engagement;

c. addressing significant findings and issues arising during the engagement, considering their significance, and modifying the planned approach appropriately; and

d. identifying matters for consultation or consideration by engagement team members with appropriate levels of skill and proficiency in auditing, specialists, or both during the engagement.

5.40 A review of the work performed includes consideration of whether

a. the work has been performed in accordance with professional standards and applicable legal and regulatory requirements;

b. significant findings and issues have been raised for further consideration;

c. appropriate consultations have taken place and the resulting conclusions have been documented and implemented;

d. the nature, timing, and extent of the work performed is appropriate and without need for revision;

e. the work performed supports the conclusions reached and is appropriately documented;

f. the evidence obtained is sufficient and appropriate to support the report; and

g. the objectives of the engagement procedures have been achieved.

5.41 In the case of a sole proprietor, the requirement for a second auditor to review work performed and related documentation may be achieved through alternative procedures.

Monitoring of Quality

Requirements: Monitoring of Quality

5.42 The audit organization should establish policies and procedures for monitoring its system of quality control.

5.43 The audit organization should perform monitoring procedures that enable it to assess compliance with professional standards and quality control policies and procedures for GAGAS engagements. Individuals performing monitoring should have sufficient expertise and authority within the audit organization.

5.44 The audit organization should analyze and summarize the results of its monitoring process at least annually, with identification of any systemic or repetitive issues needing improvement, along with recommendations for corrective action. The audit organization should communicate to the relevant engagement partner or director, and other appropriate personnel, any deficiencies noted during the monitoring process and recommend appropriate remedial action. This

Chapter 5: Quality Control and Peer Review

communication should be sufficient to enable the audit organization and appropriate personnel to take prompt corrective action related to deficiencies, when necessary, in accordance with their defined roles and responsibilities. Information communicated should include the following:

a. a description of the monitoring procedures performed;

b. the conclusions reached from the monitoring procedures; and

c. when relevant, a description of systemic, repetitive, or other deficiencies and of the actions taken to resolve those deficiencies.

5.45 The audit organization should evaluate the effects of deficiencies noted during monitoring of the audit organization's system of quality control to determine and implement appropriate actions to address the deficiencies. This evaluation should include assessments to determine if the deficiencies noted indicate that the audit organization's system of quality control is insufficient to provide it with reasonable assurance that it complies with professional standards and applicable legal and regulatory requirements, and that accordingly the reports that the audit organization issues are not appropriate in the circumstances.

5.46 The audit organization should establish policies and procedures that require retention of engagement documentation for a period of time sufficient to permit those performing monitoring procedures and peer review of the organization to evaluate its compliance with its system of quality control or for a longer period if required by law or regulation.

Application Guidance: Monitoring of Quality

5.47 Monitoring of quality is a process comprising an ongoing consideration and evaluation of the audit organization's system of quality control, including inspection of engagement documentation and reports for a selection of completed engagements. The purpose of monitoring is to provide management of the audit organization with reasonable assurance that (1) the policies and procedures related to the system of quality control are suitably designed and operating effectively in practice and (2) auditors have followed professional standards and applicable legal and regulatory requirements.

Chapter 5: Quality Control and Peer Review

5.48 Monitoring is most effective when performed by persons who do not have responsibility for the specific activity being monitored.

5.49 Monitoring procedures will vary based on the audit organization's facts and circumstances.

5.50 Ongoing consideration and evaluation of the audit organization's system of quality control may identify circumstances that necessitate changes to, or improve compliance with, the audit organization's policies and procedures to provide the audit organization with reasonable assurance that its system of quality control is effective.

5.51 Ongoing consideration and evaluation of the audit organization's system of quality control may include matters such as the following:

    a. review of selected administrative and human resource records pertaining to the quality control elements;

    b. review of engagement documentation and reports;

    c. discussions with the audit organization's personnel;

    d. determination of corrective actions to be taken and improvements to be made in the system, including providing feedback on the audit organization's policies and procedures relating to education and training;

    e. communication to appropriate audit organization personnel of weaknesses identified in the system, in the level of understanding of the system, or compliance with the system; and

    f. follow-up by appropriate audit organization personnel so that necessary modifications are promptly made to the quality control policies and procedures.

5.52 Monitoring procedures may also include an assessment of the following:

    a. the appropriateness of the audit organization's guidance materials and any practice aids;

b. new developments in professional standards and applicable legal and regulatory requirements and how they are reflected in the audit organization's policies and procedures, when appropriate;

c. written affirmation of compliance with policies and procedures on independence;

d. the effectiveness of staff training;

e. decisions related to acceptance and continuance of relationships with audited entities and specific engagements; and

f. audit organization personnel's understanding of the organization's quality control policies and procedures and implementation thereof.

5.53 Reviews of the work by engagement team members prior to the date of the report are not monitoring procedures.

5.54 The extent of inspection procedures depends, in part, on the existence and effectiveness of the other monitoring procedures. Inspection is a retrospective evaluation of the adequacy of the audit organization's quality control policies and procedures, its personnel's understanding of those policies and procedures, and the extent of the audit organization's compliance with them. The nature of inspection procedures varies based on the audit organization's quality control policies and procedures and the effectiveness and results of other monitoring procedures.

5.55 The inspection of a selection of completed engagements may be performed on a cyclical basis. The manner in which the inspection cycle is organized, including the timing of selection of individual engagements, depends on many factors, such as the following:

a. the size of the audit organization;

b. the number and geographical location of offices;

c. the results of previous monitoring procedures;

d. the degree of authority of both personnel and office (for example, whether individual offices are authorized to conduct their own inspections or whether only the head office may conduct them);

e. the nature and complexity of the audit organization's practice and structure; and

f. the risks associated with entities audited by the audit organization and specific engagements.

5.56 The inspection process involves the selection of individual engagements, some of which may be selected without prior notification to the engagement team. In determining the scope of the inspections, the audit organization may take into account the scope or conclusions of a peer review or regulatory inspections.

5.57 Reporting of identified deficiencies to individuals other than the relevant engagement partner or director need not include identifying the specific engagements concerned, unless such identification is necessary for individuals other than the engagement partner or director to properly discharge their responsibilities.

5.58 Whether engagement documentation is in paper, electronic, or other form, the integrity, accessibility, and retrievability of the underlying information could be compromised if the documentation is altered, added to, or deleted without the auditors' knowledge or if the documentation is lost or damaged.

5.59 Appropriate documentation relating to monitoring may include, for example, the following:

a. monitoring procedures, including the procedure for selecting completed engagements to be inspected;

b. a record of the evaluation of the following:

(1) adherence to professional standards and applicable legal and regulatory requirements,

(2) whether the system of quality control has been appropriately designed and is effectively implemented and operating, and

(3) whether the audit organization's quality control policies and procedures have been appropriately applied so that the reports that are issued by the audit organization are appropriate in the circumstances; and

Chapter 5: Quality Control and Peer Review

c. identification of the deficiencies noted, an evaluation of their effect, and the basis for determining whether and what further action is necessary.

External Peer Review

Requirements: General

5.60 Each audit organization conducting engagements in accordance with GAGAS must obtain an external peer review conducted by reviewers independent of the audit organization being reviewed. The peer review should be sufficient in scope to provide a reasonable basis for determining whether, for the period under review, (1) the reviewed audit organization's system of quality control was suitably designed and (2) the organization is complying with its quality control system so that it has reasonable assurance that it is performing and reporting in conformity with professional standards and applicable legal and regulatory requirements in all material respects.

5.61 Audit organizations affiliated with one of the following recognized organizations should comply with the respective organization's peer review requirements and the requirements listed throughout paragraphs 5.66 through 5.80.

 a. American Institute of Certified Public Accountants

 b. Council of the Inspectors General on Integrity and Efficiency

 c. Association of Local Government Auditors

 d. International Organization of Supreme Audit Institutions

 e. National State Auditors Association

5.62 Any audit organization not affiliated with an organization listed in paragraph 5.61 should meet the minimum GAGAS peer review requirements throughout paragraphs 5.66 through 5.94.

Application Guidance: General

5.63 Each audit organization has discretion in selecting and accepting its peer review teams. Auditors in governments or jurisdictions without access to established peer review programs may engage other auditors,

Chapter 5: Quality Control and Peer Review

including public accounting firms, to conduct their peer reviews. If access to an established peer review program is not available, auditors may organize regional programs with other auditors.

5.64 In cases of unusual difficulty or hardship, extensions of the deadlines for submitting peer review reports exceeding 3 months beyond the due date may be granted by the entity that administers the peer review program with the concurrence of GAO.

5.65 Some audit organizations may be subject to or required to follow a peer review program of a recognized organization. Other audit organizations may follow a specific peer review program voluntarily. In instances where the audit organization follows a recognized organization's peer review program voluntarily, the use of such a peer review program means compliance with the recognized organization's entire peer review process, including, where applicable, standards for administering, performing, and reporting on peer reviews, oversight procedures, training, and related guidance materials.

Requirements: Assessment of Peer Review Risk

5.66 The peer review team should perform an assessment of peer review risk to help determine the number and types of engagements to select for review.

5.67 Based on the risk assessment, the peer review team should select engagements that provide a reasonable cross section of all types of work subject to the reviewed audit organization's quality control system, including one or more engagements conducted in accordance with GAGAS.

Application Guidance: Assessment of Peer Review Risk

5.68 Peer review risk is the risk that the review team

  a. fails to identify significant weaknesses in the reviewed audit organization's system of quality control for its auditing practice, its lack of compliance with that system, or a combination thereof;

  b. issues an inappropriate opinion on the reviewed audit organization's system of quality control for its auditing practice, its compliance with that system, or a combination thereof; or

Chapter 5: Quality Control and Peer Review

c. makes an inappropriate decision about the matters to be included in, or excluded from, the peer review report.

5.69 A selection approach that provides a cross section of all types of work is generally applicable to audit organizations that conduct a small number of GAGAS engagements in relation to other types of engagements. In these cases, one or more GAGAS engagements may represent more than what would be selected when looking at a cross section of the audit organization's work as a whole. Some audit organizations conduct audit and attestation work in a number of functional areas. For example, an organization may conduct financial audits, attestation engagements, reviews of financial statements, and performance audits. The peer review team may consider reviewing a sample of engagements from each of the major functional areas included within the scope of the review.

5.70 A peer review is designed to test significant risk areas where it is possible that engagements are not being conducted, reported on, or both in conformity with professional standards and applicable legal and regulatory requirements in all material respects. A peer review is not designed to test every engagement, compliance with every professional standard, or every detailed component of the audit organization's system of quality control.

5.71 Examples of the factors that may be considered when performing an assessment of risk for selecting engagements for peer review include

a. scope of the engagements, including size of the audited entity or engagements covering multiple locations;

b. functional area or type of government program;

c. types of engagements conducted, including the extent of nonaudit services provided to audited entities;

d. personnel (including use of new personnel or personnel not routinely assigned the types of engagements conducted);

e. initial engagements;

f. familiarity resulting from a long-standing relationship with the audited entity;

g. political sensitivity of the engagements;

h. budget constraints faced by the audit organization that could negatively affect engagement quality;

i. results of the peer review team's review of the design of system of quality control;

j. results of the audit organization's monitoring process; and

k. overall risk tolerance within the audit organization that could negatively affect engagement quality.

Requirements: Peer Review Report Ratings

5.72 The peer review team should use professional judgment in deciding on the type of peer review rating to issue; the ratings are as follows:

a. Peer review rating of pass: A conclusion that the audit organization's system of quality control has been suitably designed and complied with to provide the audit organization with reasonable assurance of performing and reporting in conformity with professional standards and applicable legal and regulatory requirements in all material respects.

b. Peer review rating of pass with deficiencies: A conclusion that the audit organization's system of quality control has been suitably designed and complied with to provide the audit organization with reasonable assurance of performing and reporting in conformity with professional standards and applicable legal and regulatory requirements in all material respects with the exception of a certain deficiency or deficiencies described in the report.

c. Peer review rating of fail: A conclusion, based on the significant deficiencies described in the report, that the audit organization's system of quality control is not suitably designed to provide the audit organization with reasonable assurance of performing and reporting in conformity with professional standards and applicable legal and regulatory requirements in all material respects, or that the audit organization has not complied with its

Chapter 5: Quality Control and Peer Review

system of quality control to provide the audit organization with reasonable assurance of performing and reporting in conformity with professional standards and applicable legal and regulatory requirements in all material respects.

5.73 The peer review team should determine the type of peer review rating to issue based on the observed matters' importance to the audit organization's system of quality control as a whole and the nature, causes, patterns, and pervasiveness of those matters. The matters should be assessed both alone and in aggregate.

5.74 The peer review team should aggregate and systematically evaluate any observed matters (circumstances that warrant further consideration by the peer review team) and document its evaluation.[37] The peer review team should perform its evaluation and issue report ratings as follows:

a. If the peer review team's evaluation of observed matters does not identify any findings (more than a remote possibility that the reviewed audit organization would not perform, report, or both in conformity with professional standards and applicable legal and regulatory requirements), or identifies findings that are not considered to be deficiencies, the peer review team issues a pass rating.

b. If the peer review team's evaluation of findings identified deficiencies but did not identify any significant deficiencies, the peer review team issues a pass with deficiencies rating and communicates the deficiencies in its report.

c. If the peer review team's evaluation of deficiencies identified significant deficiencies, the peer review team issues a fail rating and communicates the deficiencies and significant deficiencies in its report.

---

[37]See fig. 3 for a flowchart on developing peer review communications for observed matters in accordance with GAGAS.

Chapter 5: Quality Control and Peer Review

Application Guidance: Peer Review Report Ratings

5.75 Deficiencies are findings that because of their nature, causes, pattern, or pervasiveness, including their relative importance to the audit organization's system of quality control taken as a whole, could create a situation in which the audit organization would not have reasonable assurance of performing, reporting, or both in conformity with professional standards and applicable legal and regulatory requirements in one or more important respects.

5.76 Significant deficiencies are one or more deficiencies that the peer review team concludes result from a condition in the audit organization's system of quality control or compliance with that system such that the system taken as a whole does not provide reasonable assurance of performing, reporting, or both in conformity with professional standards and applicable legal and regulatory requirements.

Requirements: Availability of the Peer Review Report to the Public

5.77 An external audit organization should make its most recent peer review report publicly available. If a separate communication detailing findings, conclusions, and recommendations is issued, the external audit organization is not required to make that communication publicly available. An internal audit organization that reports internally to management and those charged with governance should provide a copy of its peer review report to those charged with governance.

5.78 An external audit organization should satisfy the publication requirement for its peer review report by posting the report on a publicly available website or to a publicly available file. Alternatively, if neither of these options is available, then the audit organization should use the same mechanism it uses to make other reports or documents public.

5.79 Because information in peer review reports may be relevant to decisions on procuring audit services, an audit organization seeking to enter into a contract to conduct an engagement in accordance with GAGAS should provide the following to the party contracting for such services when requested:

Chapter 5: Quality Control and Peer Review

a. the audit organization's most recent peer review report and

b. any subsequent peer review reports received during the period of the contract.

5.80 Auditors who are using another audit organization's work should request a copy of that organization's most recent peer review report, and the organization should provide this document when it is requested.

Application Guidance: Availability of the Peer Review Report to the Public

5.81 To help the public understand the peer review reports, an audit organization may include a description of the peer review process and how it applies to its organization. Examples of additional information that audit organizations may include to help users understand the meaning of the peer review report follow:

a. Explanation of the peer review process.

b. Description of the audit organization's system of quality control.

c. Explanation of the relationship of the peer review results to the audited organization's work.

d. If a peer review report is issued with a rating of pass with deficiencies or fail, explanation of the reviewed audit organization's plan for improving quality controls and the status of the improvements.

Additional Requirements for Audit Organizations Not Affiliated with Recognized Organizations

Requirement: Peer Review Scope

5.82 The peer review team should include the following elements in the scope of the peer review:

a. review of the audit organization's design of, and compliance with, quality control and related policies and procedures;

> b. consideration of the adequacy and results of the audit organization's internal monitoring procedures;
>
> c. review of selected audit reports and related documentation and, if applicable, documentation related to selected terminated engagements prepared in accordance with paragraph 5.25, if any terminated engagements are selected from the universe of engagements used for the peer review sample;
>
> d. review of prior peer review reports, if applicable;
>
> e. review of other documents necessary for assessing compliance with standards, for example, independence documentation, CPE records, and relevant human resource management files; and
>
> f. interviews with selected members of the audit organization's personnel in various roles to assess their understanding of and compliance with relevant quality control policies and procedures.

Application Guidance: Peer Review Scope

5.83 Review of documentation related to terminated engagements can provide information on the audit organization's response to threats to independence. For example, the documentation may include information on whether an engagement was terminated as a result of an undue influence from outside the audit organization.

> ### Requirement: Peer Review Intervals
>
> **5.84** An audit organization not already subject to a peer review requirement should obtain an external peer review at least once every 3 years. The audit organization should obtain its first peer review covering a review period ending no later than 3 years from the date an audit organization begins its first engagement in accordance with GAGAS.

Application Guidance: Peer Review Intervals

5.85 The period under review in a peer review generally covers 1 year.

Requirement: Written Agreement for Peer Review

5.86 The peer review team and the reviewed audit organization should incorporate their basic agreement on the peer review into a written agreement. The written agreement should be drafted by the peer review team, reviewed by the reviewed audit organization to ensure that it accurately describes the agreement between the parties, and signed by the authorized representatives of both the peer review team and the reviewed audit organization prior to the initiation of work under the agreement. The written agreement should state that the peer review will be conducted in accordance with GAGAS peer review requirements.

Application Guidance: Written Agreement for Peer Review

5.87 The written agreement is meant to ensure mutual consent on the fundamental aspects of the peer review and to avoid any potential misunderstandings. The written agreement may address the following:

a. scope of the peer review;

b. staffing and time frame;

c. compensation for conducting the peer review, if applicable;

d. preliminary findings, if applicable;

e. reporting results;

f. administrative matters; and

g. access to audit documentation.

5.88 The peer review team is responsible for ensuring that the peer review is conducted in accordance with GAGAS peer review requirements.

Chapter 5: Quality Control and Peer Review

Requirement: Peer Review Team

5.89 The peer review team should meet the following criteria:

a. The review team collectively has adequate professional competence and knowledge of GAGAS and government auditing.

b. The organization conducting the peer review and individual review team members are independent (as defined in GAGAS) of the audit organization being reviewed, its personnel, and the engagements selected for the peer review.[38]

c. The review team collectively has sufficient knowledge to conduct a peer review.

Application Guidance: Peer Review Team

5.90 Peer review knowledge and professional competence may be obtained from on-the-job training, training courses, or a combination of both. Having individuals on the peer review team with prior experience on a peer review or internal inspection team is desirable.

Requirement: Report Content

5.91 The peer review team should prepare one or more written reports communicating the results of the peer review, which collectively include the following elements:

a. a description of the scope of the peer review, including any limitations;

b. a rating concluding on whether the system of quality control of the reviewed audit organization was adequately designed and complied with during the period reviewed and would provide the audit organization with reasonable assurance that it conformed to professional standards and applicable legal and regulatory

---

[38] See paras. 3.18 through 3.108 for discussion of independence.

requirements;

c. specification of the professional standards and applicable legal and regulatory requirements to which the reviewed audit organization is being held;

d. reference to a separate written communication, if issued under the peer review program;

e. a statement that the peer review was conducted in accordance with GAGAS peer review requirements; and

f. a detailed description of the findings, conclusions, and recommendations related to any deficiencies or significant deficiencies identified in the review.

Application Guidance: Report Content

5.92 When the scope of the peer review is limited by conditions that preclude the application of one or more peer review procedures considered necessary in the circumstances and the peer review team cannot accomplish the objectives of those procedures through alternative procedures, the report can be modified by including a statement in the report's scope paragraph, body, and opinion paragraph. The statement describes the relationship of the excluded engagement(s) or functional area(s) to the reviewed audit organization's full scope of practice as a whole and system of quality control and the effects of the exclusion on the scope and results of the review.

Requirements: Audit Organization's Response to the Peer Review Report

5.93 If the reviewed audit organization receives a report with a peer review rating of pass with deficiencies or fail, the reviewed audit organization should respond in writing to the deficiencies or significant deficiencies and related recommendations identified in the report.

5.94 With respect to each deficiency or significant deficiency in the report, the reviewed audit organization should describe in its letter of response the corrective actions already taken, target dates for planned corrective actions, or both.

Application Guidance: Audit Organization's Response to the Peer Review Report

5.95 When an audit organization receives a peer review rating of pass with deficiencies or fail that relates to its GAGAS engagements, critical evaluation of the design and implementation of the system of quality control is a factor in determining the audit organization's ability to accept and perform future GAGAS engagements.

Figure 3: Developing Peer Review Communications for Observed Matters in Accordance with Generally Accepted Government Auditing Standards

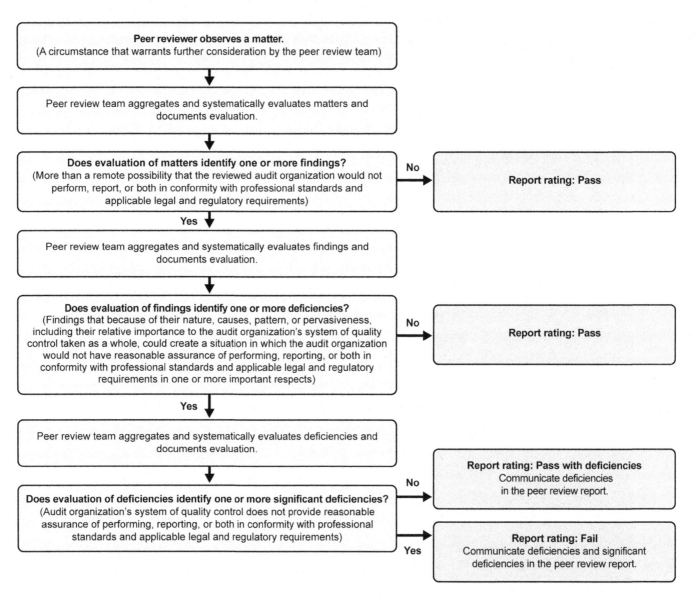

Source: GAO. | GAO-18-568G

Chapter 6: Standards for Financial Audits

6.01 This chapter contains requirements and guidance for conducting and reporting on financial audits conducted in accordance with generally accepted government auditing standards (GAGAS). GAGAS incorporates by reference the American Institute of Certified Public Accountants' (AICPA) Statements on Auditing Standards (SAS).[39] All sections of the SAS are incorporated, including the introduction, objectives, definitions, requirements, and application material. GAGAS does not incorporate the AICPA Code of Professional Conduct by reference but recognizes that certain certified public accountants (CPA) may use or may be required to use the code in conjunction with GAGAS.[40] For financial audits conducted in accordance with GAGAS, the requirements and guidance in the incorporated SAS and this chapter apply. The requirements and guidance contained in chapters 1 through 5 also apply.

Additional GAGAS Requirements for Conducting Financial Audits

Compliance with Standards

Requirement: Compliance with Standards

6.02 GAGAS establishes requirements for financial audits in addition to the requirements in the AICPA SAS. Auditors should comply with these additional requirements, along with the AICPA requirements for financial audits, when citing GAGAS in financial audit reports.

Application Guidance: Compliance with Standards

6.03 Standards used in conjunction with GAGAS require the auditors to apply the concept of materiality appropriately in planning and performing the audit.[41] Additional considerations may apply to GAGAS engagements

---

[39]See para. 2.13 and the AICPA *Codification of Statements on Auditing Standards* (AU-C) for additional discussion of the relationship between GAGAS and other professional standards.

[40]See para. 2.14 for a discussion of the AICPA Code of Professional Conduct.

[41]See AU-C section 320, *Materiality in Planning and Performing an Audit* (AICPA, *Professional Standards*).

Chapter 6: Standards for Financial Audits

that concern government entities or entities that receive government awards. For example, for engagements conducted in accordance with GAGAS, auditors may find it appropriate to use lower materiality levels than those used in non-GAGAS audits because of the public accountability of government entities and entities receiving government funding, various legal and regulatory requirements, and the visibility and sensitivity of government programs.

Licensing and Certification

Requirements: Licensing and Certification

6.04 Auditors engaged to conduct financial audits in the United States who do not work for a government audit organization should be licensed CPAs, persons working for licensed certified public accounting firms, or licensed accountants in states that have multiclass licensing systems that recognize licensed accountants other than CPAs.

6.05 Auditors engaged to conduct financial audits of entities operating outside of the United States who do not work for a government audit organization should meet the qualifications indicated in paragraph 6.04, have certifications that meet all applicable national and international standards and serve in their respective countries as the functional equivalent of CPAs in the United States, or work for nongovernment audit organizations that are the functional equivalent of licensed certified public accounting firms in the United States.

Auditor Communication

Requirements: Auditor Communication

6.06 If the law or regulation requiring an audit specifically identifies the entities to be audited, auditors should communicate pertinent information that in the auditors' professional judgment needs to be communicated both to individuals contracting for or requesting the audit and to those legislative committees, if any, that have ongoing oversight responsibilities for the audited entity.

6.07 If the identity of those charged with governance is not clearly evident, auditors should document the process followed and

Chapter 6: Standards for Financial Audits

> conclusions reached in identifying the appropriate individuals to receive the required communications.

Application Guidance: Auditor Communication

6.08 One example of a law or regulation requiring an audit that does not specifically identify the entities to be audited is the Single Audit Act Amendments of 1996.

6.09 For some matters, early communication to management or those charged with governance may be important because of the relative significance and the urgency for corrective follow-up action.[42] Further, early communication is important to allow management to take prompt corrective action to prevent further occurrences when a control deficiency results in identified or suspected noncompliance with provisions of laws, regulations, contracts, and grant agreements or identified or suspected instances of fraud. When a deficiency is communicated early, the reporting requirements and application guidance in paragraphs 6.39 through 6.49 still apply.

6.10 Because the governance structures of government entities and organizations can vary widely, it may not always be clearly evident who is charged with key governance functions. The process for identifying those charged with governance includes evaluating the organizational structure for directing and controlling operations to achieve the audited entity's objectives and how the audited entity delegates authority and establishes accountability for management.

Results of Previous Engagements

Requirement: Results of Previous Engagements

6.11 When planning the audit, auditors should ask management of the audited entity to identify previous audits, attestation engagements, and other studies that directly relate to the objectives of the audit, including whether related recommendations have been implemented. Auditors should evaluate whether the audited entity has taken appropriate

---

[42]See AU-C section 265, *Communicating Internal Control Related Matters Identified in an Audit* (AICPA, *Professional Standards*).

corrective action to address findings and recommendations from previous engagements that could have a significant effect on the subject matter. Auditors should use this information in assessing risk and determining the nature, timing, and extent of current audit work and determining the extent to which testing the implementation of the corrective actions is applicable to the current audit objectives.

Investigations or Legal Proceedings

Requirement: Investigations or Legal Proceedings

6.12 Auditors should inquire of management of the audited entity whether any investigations or legal proceedings have been initiated or are in process with respect to the period under audit, and should evaluate the effect of initiated or in-process investigations or legal proceedings on the current audit.

Application Guidance: Investigations or Legal Proceedings

6.13 Laws, regulations, or policies may require auditors to communicate indications of certain types of fraud or noncompliance with provisions of laws, regulations, contracts, and grant agreements to law enforcement or investigatory authorities before performing additional audit procedures.

6.14 Avoiding interference with investigations or legal proceedings is important in pursuing indications of fraud and noncompliance with provisions of laws, regulations, contracts, and grant agreements. In some cases, it may be appropriate for the auditors to work with investigators or legal authorities or to withdraw from or defer further work on the engagement or a portion of the engagement to avoid interfering with an ongoing investigation or legal proceeding.

Noncompliance with Provisions of Laws, Regulations, Contracts, and Grant Agreements

Requirement: Noncompliance with Provisions of Laws, Regulations, Contracts, and Grant Agreements

6.15 Auditors should extend the AICPA requirements concerning consideration of noncompliance with laws and regulations to include

Chapter 6: Standards for Financial Audits

> consideration of noncompliance with provisions of contracts and grant agreements.[43]

Application Guidance: Noncompliance with Provisions of Laws, Regulations, Contracts, and Grant Agreements

6.16 Government programs are subject to provisions of many laws, regulations, contracts, and grant agreements. At the same time, these provisions' significance within the context of the audit objectives varies widely, depending on the objectives of the audit. Auditors may consult with their legal counsel to (1) determine those laws and regulations that are significant to the audit objectives, (2) design tests of compliance with laws and regulations, and (3) evaluate the results of those tests. Auditors also may consult with their legal counsel when audit objectives require testing compliance with provisions of contracts or grant agreements. Depending on the circumstances of the audit, auditors may consult with others, such as investigative staff, other audit organizations or government entities that provided professional services to the audited entity, or applicable law enforcement authorities, to obtain information on compliance matters.

Findings

> **Requirements: Findings**
>
> **6.17** When auditors identify findings, they should plan and perform procedures to develop the criteria, condition, cause, and effect of the findings to the extent that these elements are relevant and necessary to achieve the audit objectives.
>
> **6.18** Auditors should consider internal control deficiencies in their evaluation of identified findings when developing the cause element of the identified findings.

---

[43]See AU-C section 250, *Consideration of Laws and Regulations in an Audit of Financial Statements* (AICPA, *Professional Standards*).

Application Guidance: Findings

6.19 Findings may involve deficiencies in internal control; noncompliance with provisions of laws, regulations, contracts, and grant agreements; or instances of fraud.

6.20 Given the concept of accountability for use of public resources and government authority, evaluating internal control in a government environment may also include considering internal control deficiencies that result in waste or abuse. Because the determination of waste and abuse is subjective, auditors are not required to perform specific procedures to detect waste or abuse in financial audits. However, auditors may consider whether and how to communicate such matters if they become aware of them. Auditors may also discover that waste or abuse are indicative of fraud or noncompliance with provisions of laws, regulations, contracts, and grant agreements.

6.21 Waste is the act of using or expending resources carelessly, extravagantly, or to no purpose. Importantly, waste can include activities that do not include abuse and does not necessarily involve a violation of law. Rather, waste relates primarily to mismanagement, inappropriate actions, and inadequate oversight.

6.22 The following are examples of waste, depending on the facts and circumstances:

   a. Making travel choices that are contrary to existing travel policies or are unnecessarily extravagant or expensive.

   b. Making procurement or vendor selections that are contrary to existing policies or are unnecessarily extravagant or expensive.

6.23 Abuse is behavior that is deficient or improper when compared with behavior that a prudent person would consider reasonable and necessary business practice given the facts and circumstances, but excludes fraud and noncompliance with provisions of laws, regulations, contracts, and grant agreements. Abuse also includes misuse of authority or position for personal financial interests or those of an immediate or close family member or business associate.

6.24 The following are examples of abuse, depending on the facts and circumstances:

a. Creating unneeded overtime.

b. Requesting staff to perform personal errands or work tasks for a supervisor or manager.

c. Misusing the official's position for personal gain (including actions that could be perceived by an objective third party with knowledge of the relevant information as improperly benefiting an official's personal financial interests or those of an immediate or close family member; a general partner; an organization for which the official serves as an officer, director, trustee, or employee; or an organization with which the official is negotiating concerning future employment).

6.25 Criteria: For inclusion in findings, criteria may include the laws, regulations, contracts, grant agreements, standards, measures, expected performance, defined business practices, and benchmarks against which performance is compared or evaluated. Criteria identify the required or desired state or expectation with respect to the program or operation. Criteria provide a context for evaluating evidence and understanding the findings, conclusions, and recommendations in the report. In a financial audit, the applicable financial reporting framework, such as generally accepted accounting principles, represents one set of criteria.

6.26 Condition: Condition is a situation that exists. The condition is determined and documented during the audit.

6.27 Cause: The cause is the factor or factors responsible for the difference between the condition and the criteria, and may also serve as a basis for recommendations for corrective actions. Common factors include poorly designed policies, procedures, or criteria; inconsistent, incomplete, or incorrect implementation; or factors beyond the control of program management. Auditors may assess whether the evidence provides a reasonable and convincing argument for why the stated cause is the key factor contributing to the difference between the condition and the criteria.

6.28 Effect or potential effect: The effect or potential effect is the outcome or consequence resulting from the difference between the condition and the criteria. When the audit objectives include identifying the actual or potential consequences of a condition that varies (either positively or negatively) from the criteria identified in the audit, effect is a measure of those consequences. Effect or potential effect may be used to demonstrate the need for corrective action in response to identified problems or relevant risks.

6.29 Regardless of the type of finding identified, the cause of a finding may relate to one or more underlying internal control deficiencies. Depending on the magnitude of impact, likelihood of occurrence, and nature of the deficiency, the deficiency could be a significant deficiency or material weakness in a financial audit.[44]

6.30 Considering internal control in the context of a comprehensive internal control framework, such as *Standards for Internal Control in the Federal Government* or *Internal Control—Integrated Framework*,[45] can help auditors to determine whether underlying internal control deficiencies exist as the root cause of findings. Identifying these deficiencies can help provide the basis for developing meaningful recommendations for corrective actions.

Audit Documentation

Requirements: Audit Documentation

6.31 Auditors should document supervisory review, before the report release date, of the evidence that supports the findings and conclusions contained in the audit report.

6.32 Auditors should document any departures from the GAGAS requirements and the effect on the audit and on the auditors' conclusions when the audit is not in compliance with applicable GAGAS requirements because of law, regulation, scope limitations, restrictions on access to records, or other issues affecting the audit.

---

[44] See AU-C section 265, *Communicating Internal Control Related Matters Identified in an Audit* (AICPA, *Professional Standards*).

[45] Para. .A16 of AU-C section 940, *An Audit of Internal Control Over Financial Reporting That Is Integrated With an Audit of Financial Statements* (AICPA, *Professional* Standards) indicates that the Committee of Sponsoring Organizations of the Treadway Commission's *Internal Control—Integrated Framework* and *Standards for Internal Control in the Federal Government* (GAO-14-704G) provide suitable and available criteria against which management may evaluate and report on the effectiveness of the entity's internal control over financial reporting. *Standards for Internal Control in the Federal Government* may be adopted by entities beyond those federal entities for which it is legally required, such as state, local, and quasi-governmental entities, as well as other federal entities and not-for-profit organizations, as a framework for an internal control system.

Chapter 6: Standards for Financial Audits

Application Guidance: Audit Documentation

6.33 When documenting departures from the GAGAS requirements, the audit documentation requirements apply to departures from unconditional requirements and from presumptively mandatory requirements when alternative procedures performed in the circumstances were not sufficient to achieve the objectives of the requirements.

Availability of Individuals and Documentation

Requirement: Availability of Individuals and Documentation

6.34 Subject to applicable provisions of laws and regulations, auditors should make appropriate individuals and audit documentation available upon request and in a timely manner to other auditors or reviewers.

Application Guidance: Availability of Individuals and Documentation

6.35 Underlying GAGAS audits is the premise that audit organizations in federal, state, and local governments and public accounting firms engaged to conduct financial audits in accordance with GAGAS cooperate in auditing programs of common interest so that auditors may use others' work and avoid duplication of efforts. The use of auditors' work by other auditors may be facilitated by contractual arrangements for GAGAS audits that provide for full and timely access to appropriate individuals and to audit documentation.

Additional GAGAS Requirements for Reporting on Financial Audits

Reporting the Auditors' Compliance with GAGAS

Requirement: Reporting the Auditors' Compliance with GAGAS

6.36 When auditors comply with all applicable GAGAS requirements, they should include a statement in the audit report that they conducted the audit in accordance with GAGAS.[46]

Application Guidance: Reporting the Auditors' Compliance with GAGAS

6.37 Because GAGAS incorporates by reference the AICPA's financial audit standards, GAGAS does not require auditors to cite compliance with the AICPA standards when citing compliance with GAGAS. GAGAS does not prohibit auditors from issuing a separate report conforming only to the requirements of the AICPA or other standards.[47]

6.38 When disclaiming an opinion on a financial audit, auditors may revise the statement that the auditor was engaged to audit the financial statements.[48] For example, auditors may state that they were engaged to conduct the audit in accordance with GAGAS or that the auditors' work was conducted in accordance with GAGAS, depending on whether the use of GAGAS is required or voluntary. Determining how to revise this statement is a matter of professional judgment.

---

[46] See paras. 2.16 through 2.19 for information on the GAGAS compliance statement.

[47] See AU-C section 700, *Forming an Opinion and Reporting on Financial Statements* (AICPA, *Professional Standards*).

[48] See AU-C section 705, *Modifications to the Opinion in the Independent Auditor's Report* (AICPA, *Professional Standards*).

Reporting on Internal Control; Compliance with Provisions of Laws, Regulations, Contracts, and Grant Agreements; and Instances of Fraud

Requirements: Reporting on Internal Control; Compliance with Provisions of Laws, Regulations, Contracts, and Grant Agreements; and Instances of Fraud

6.39 Auditors should report on internal control and compliance with provisions of laws, regulations, contracts, or grant agreements regardless of whether they identify internal control deficiencies or instances of noncompliance.

6.40 When providing an opinion or a disclaimer on financial statements, auditors should report as findings any significant deficiencies or material weaknesses in internal control over financial reporting that the auditors identified based on the engagement work performed.

6.41 Auditors should include in their report on internal control or compliance the relevant information about noncompliance and fraud when auditors, based on sufficient, appropriate evidence, identify or suspect

   a. noncompliance with provisions of laws, regulations, contracts, or grant agreements that has a material effect on the financial statements or other financial data significant to the audit objectives or

   b. fraud that is material, either quantitatively or qualitatively, to the financial statements or other financial data significant to the audit objectives.

6.42 Auditors should include either in the same or in separate report(s) a description of the scope of the auditors' testing of internal control over financial reporting and of compliance with provisions of laws, regulations, contracts, and grant agreements. Auditors should also state in the report(s) whether the tests they performed provided sufficient, appropriate evidence to support opinions on the effectiveness of internal control and on compliance with provisions of laws, regulations, contracts, and grant agreements.

6.43 If auditors report separately (including separate reports bound in the same document) on internal control over financial reporting and on compliance with provisions of laws, regulations, contracts, and grant agreements, they should include a reference in the audit report on the financial statements to those additional reports. They should also state in the audit report that the reports on internal control over financial reporting and on compliance with provisions of laws, regulations, contracts, and grant agreements are an integral part of a GAGAS audit in considering the audited entity's internal control over financial reporting and compliance. If separate reports are used, the auditors should make the report on internal control and compliance available to users in the same manner as the financial audit report to which it relates.

6.44 Auditors should communicate in writing to audited entity officials when

a. identified or suspected noncompliance with provisions of laws, regulations, contracts, or grant agreements comes to the auditor's attention during the course of an audit that has an effect on the financial statements or other financial data significant to the audit objectives that is less than material but warrants the attention of those charged with governance or

b. the auditor has obtained evidence of identified or suspected instances of fraud that have an effect on the financial statements or other financial data significant to the audit objectives that are less than material but warrant the attention of those charged with governance.

Application Guidance: Reporting on Internal Control; Compliance with Provisions of Laws, Regulations, Contracts, and Grant Agreements; and Instances of Fraud

6.45 The GAGAS requirement to report on internal control over financial reporting is based on the AICPA requirements to communicate in writing to those charged with governance significant deficiencies and material weaknesses in internal control over financial reporting identified during an audit. The objective of the GAGAS internal control reporting requirement for financial audits is to increase the availability of information on significant deficiencies and material weaknesses to users of financial statements other than those charged with governance.

6.46 Internal control plays an expanded role in the government sector. Given the government's accountability for public resources, assessing

Chapter 6: Standards for Financial Audits

internal control in a government environment may involve considering controls that would not be required in the private sector. In the government sector, evaluating controls that are relevant to the audit involves understanding significant controls that the audited entity designed, implemented, and operated as part of its responsibility for oversight of public resources.

6.47 The audit report on internal control and compliance with provisions of laws, regulations, contracts, and grant agreements relates only to the most recent reporting period included, when comparative financial statements are presented.

6.48 When identified or suspected noncompliance with provisions of laws, regulations, contracts, or grant agreements that does not warrant the attention of those charged with governance comes to the auditor's attention during the course of the audit, the auditors' determination of how to communicate such instances to audited entity officials is a matter of professional judgment. When identified or suspected noncompliance with provisions of laws, regulations, contracts, or grant agreements is clearly inconsequential, the auditors' determination of whether and how to communicate such instances to audited entity officials is a matter of professional judgment.

6.49 When auditors identify or suspect noncompliance with provisions of laws, regulations, contracts, or grant agreements or instances of fraud, auditors may consult with authorities or legal counsel about whether publicly reporting such information would compromise investigative or legal proceedings. Auditors may limit their public reporting to matters that would not compromise those proceedings and, for example, report only on information that is already a part of the public record.

Presenting Findings in the Audit Report

Requirements: Presenting Findings in the Audit Report

6.50 When presenting findings, auditors should develop the elements of the findings to the extent necessary to assist management or oversight officials of the audited entity in understanding the need for corrective action.

6.51 Auditors should place their findings in perspective by describing the nature and extent of the issues being reported and the extent of the work performed that resulted in the finding. To give the reader a basis for judging the prevalence and consequences of these findings, auditors should, as appropriate, relate the instances identified to the population or the number of cases examined and quantify the results in terms of dollar value or other measures. If the results cannot be projected, auditors should limit their conclusions appropriately.

Application Guidance: Presenting Findings in the Audit Report

6.52 Along with assisting management or oversight officials of the audited entity in understanding the need for corrective action, clearly developed findings assist auditors in making recommendations for corrective action. If auditors sufficiently develop the elements of a finding, they may provide recommendations for corrective action.

Reporting Findings Directly to Parties outside the Audited Entity

Requirements: Reporting Findings Directly to Parties outside the Audited Entity

6.53 Auditors should report identified or suspected noncompliance with provisions of laws, regulations, contracts, and grant agreements and instances of fraud directly to parties outside the audited entity in the following two circumstances.

  a. When audited entity management fails to satisfy legal or regulatory requirements to report such information to external parties specified in law or regulation, auditors should first communicate the failure to report such information to those charged with governance. If the audited entity still does not report this information to the specified external parties as soon as practicable after the auditors' communication with those charged with governance, then the auditors should report the information directly to the specified external parties.

  b. When audited entity management fails to take timely and appropriate steps to respond to fraud or noncompliance with provisions of laws, regulations, contracts, and grant agreements that (1) is likely to have a material effect on the subject matter and (2) involves funding received directly or indirectly from a government agency, auditors should first report management's failure to take timely and appropriate steps to those charged with governance. If the audited entity still does not take timely and appropriate steps as soon as practicable after the auditors' communication with those charged with governance, then the auditors should report the audited entity's failure to take timely and appropriate steps directly to the funding agency.

6.54 Auditors should comply with the requirements in paragraph 6.53 even if they have resigned or been dismissed from the audit prior to its completion.

6.55 Auditors should obtain sufficient, appropriate evidence, such as confirmation from outside parties, to corroborate representations by management of the audited entity that it has reported audit findings in accordance with provisions of laws, regulations, or funding agreements. When auditors are unable to do so, they should report such information directly as discussed in paragraphs 6.53 and 6.54.

Application Guidance: Reporting Findings Directly to Parties outside the Audited Entity

6.56 The reporting in paragraph 6.53 is in addition to any legal requirements to report such information directly to parties outside the audited entity.

Obtaining and Reporting the Views of Responsible Officials

Requirements: Obtaining and Reporting the Views of Responsible Officials

6.57 Auditors should obtain and report the views of responsible officials of the audited entity concerning the findings, conclusions, and recommendations in the audit report, as well as any planned corrective actions.

6.58 When auditors receive written comments from the responsible officials, they should include in their report a copy of the officials' written comments or a summary of the comments received. When the responsible officials provide oral comments only, auditors should prepare a summary of the oral comments, provide a copy of the summary to the responsible officials to verify that the comments are accurately represented, and include the summary in their report.

6.59 When the audited entity's comments are inconsistent or in conflict with the findings, conclusions, or recommendations in the draft report, the auditors should evaluate the validity of the audited entity's comments. If the auditors disagree with the comments, they should explain in the report their reasons for disagreement. Conversely, the auditors should modify their report as necessary if they find the comments valid and supported by sufficient, appropriate evidence.

6.60 If the audited entity refuses to provide comments or is unable to provide comments within a reasonable period of time, the auditors should issue the report without receiving comments from the audited entity. In such cases, the auditors should indicate in the report that the audited entity did not provide comments.

Application Guidance: Obtaining and Reporting the Views of Responsible Officials

6.61 Providing a draft report with findings for review and comment by responsible officials of the audited entity and others helps the auditors develop a report that is fair, complete, and objective. Including the views of responsible officials results in a report that presents not only the auditors' findings, conclusions, and recommendations but also the perspectives of the audited entity's responsible officials and the corrective actions they plan to take. Obtaining the comments in writing is preferred, but oral comments are acceptable. In cases in which the audited entity provides technical comments in addition to its written or oral comments on the report, auditors may disclose in the report that such comments were received. Technical comments address points of fact or are editorial in nature and do not address substantive issues, such as methodology, findings, conclusions, or recommendations.

6.62 Obtaining oral comments may be appropriate when, for example, there is a reporting date critical to meeting a user's needs; auditors have worked closely with the responsible officials throughout the engagement, and the parties are familiar with the findings and issues addressed in the draft report; or the auditors do not expect major disagreements with findings, conclusions, or recommendations in the draft report or major controversies with regard to the issues discussed in the draft report.

Reporting Confidential or Sensitive Information

Requirements: Reporting Confidential or Sensitive Information

6.63 If certain information is prohibited from public disclosure or is excluded from a report because of its confidential or sensitive nature, auditors should disclose in the report that certain information has been omitted and the circumstances that make the omission necessary.

6.64 When circumstances call for omission of certain information from the report, auditors should evaluate whether this omission could distort the audit results or conceal improper or illegal practices and revise the report language as necessary to avoid report users drawing inappropriate conclusions from the information presented.

6.65 When the audit organization is subject to public records laws, auditors should determine whether public records laws could affect the availability of classified or limited use reports and determine whether other means of communicating with management and those charged with governance would be more appropriate. Auditors use professional judgment to determine the appropriate means to communicate the omitted information to management and those charged with governance considering, among other things, whether public records laws could affect the availability of classified or limited use reports.

Application Guidance: Reporting Confidential or Sensitive Information

6.66 If the report refers to the omitted information, the reference may be general and not specific. If the omitted information is not necessary to meet the audit objectives, the report need not refer to its omission.

6.67 Certain information may be classified or may otherwise be prohibited from general disclosure by federal, state, or local laws or regulations. In such circumstances, auditors may issue a separate, classified, or limited use report containing such information and distribute the report only to persons authorized by law or regulation to receive it.

6.68 Additional circumstances associated with public safety, privacy, or security concerns could also justify the exclusion of certain information from a publicly available or widely distributed report. For example, detailed information related to computer security for a particular program may be excluded from publicly available reports because of the potential damage that misuse of this information could cause. In such circumstances, auditors may issue a limited use report containing such information and distribute the report only to those parties responsible for acting on the auditors' recommendations. In some instances, it may be appropriate to issue both a publicly available report with the sensitive information excluded and a limited use report. The auditors may consult with legal counsel regarding any requirements or other circumstances that may necessitate omitting certain information. Considering the broad public interest in the program or activity under audit assists auditors when deciding whether to exclude certain information from publicly available reports.

6.69 In cases described in paragraph 6.65, the auditors may communicate general information in a written report and communicate detailed information orally. The auditors may consult with legal counsel regarding applicable public records laws.

Distributing Reports

Requirement: Distributing Reports

6.70 Distribution of reports completed in accordance with GAGAS depends on the auditors' relationship with the audited entity and the nature of the information contained in the reports. Auditors should document any limitation on report distribution.

a. An audit organization in a government entity should distribute audit reports to those charged with governance, to the appropriate audited entity officials, and to the appropriate oversight bodies or organizations requiring or arranging for the audits. As appropriate, auditors should also distribute copies of the reports to other officials who have legal oversight authority or who may be responsible for acting on audit findings and recommendations and to others authorized to receive such reports.

b. A public accounting firm contracted to conduct an audit in accordance with GAGAS should clarify report distribution responsibilities with the engaging party. If the contracting firm is responsible for the distribution, it should reach agreement with the party contracting for the audit about which officials or organizations will receive the report and the steps being taken to make the report available to the public.

Chapter 7: Standards for Attestation Engagements and Reviews of Financial Statements

7.01 This chapter contains requirements and guidance for conducting and reporting on attestation engagements and reviews of financial statements conducted in accordance with generally accepted government auditing standards (GAGAS). For attestation engagements, GAGAS incorporates by reference the American Institute of Certified Public Accountants' (AICPA) Statements on Standards for Attestation Engagements (SSAE). For reviews of financial statements, GAGAS incorporates by reference AICPA's AR-C section 90, *Review of Financial Statements*.[49] All sections of the cited standards are incorporated, including the introduction, objectives, definitions, requirements, and application and other explanatory material. GAGAS does not incorporate the AICPA Code of Professional Conduct by reference but recognizes that certain certified public accountants (CPA) may use or may be required to use the code in conjunction with GAGAS.[50] For attestation engagements and reviews of financial statements conducted in accordance with GAGAS, the requirements and guidance in the respective incorporated standards and this chapter apply. The requirements and guidance contained in chapters 1 through 5 also apply.

7.02 An attestation engagement can provide one of three levels of service as defined by the AICPA: an examination engagement, a review engagement, or an agreed-upon procedures engagement.

7.03 The AICPA standards used in conjunction with GAGAS require auditors to establish an understanding with the audited entity regarding the services to be performed for each attestation engagement or review of financial statements. Such an understanding reduces the risk that either the auditors or the audited entity may misinterpret the needs or expectations of the other party. The understanding includes the objectives of the engagement, responsibilities of audited entity management, responsibilities of auditors, and limitations of the engagement.[51]

7.04 Auditors often conduct GAGAS engagements under a contract with a party other than the officials of the audited entity or pursuant to a third-party request. In such cases, auditors may also find it appropriate to communicate information regarding the services to be performed to the

---

[49]AICPA, *Professional Standards*.

[50]See para. 2.14 for a discussion of the AICPA Code of Professional Conduct.

[51]See para. .08 of AT-C section 205, para. .09 of AT-C section 210, and para. .14 of AT-C section 215; and para. .11 of AR-C section 90 (AICPA, *Professional Standards*).

individuals contracting for or requesting the engagement. Such an understanding can help auditors avoid any misunderstandings regarding the nature of the review or agreed-upon procedures engagement. For example, a review engagement only provides limited assurance, and as a result, auditors do not perform sufficient work to be able to develop elements of a finding or provide recommendations that are common in other types of GAGAS engagements. An agreed-upon procedures engagement does not provide an opinion or conclusion, and as a result, auditors do not perform sufficient work to be able to develop elements of a finding or provide recommendations that are common in other types of GAGAS engagements. Consequently, requesting parties may find that a different type of attestation engagement or a performance audit may provide the appropriate level of assurance to meet their needs.

Examination Engagements

Compliance with Standards

Requirement: Compliance with Standards

7.05 GAGAS establishes requirements for examination engagements in addition to the requirements for examinations contained in the AICPA's SSAEs. Auditors should comply with these additional requirements, along with the AICPA requirements for examination engagements, when citing GAGAS in their examination engagement reports.

Application Guidance: Compliance with Standards

7.06 The AICPA standards applicable to examinations require the auditors to apply the concept of materiality appropriately in planning and performing the examination. Additional considerations may apply to GAGAS engagements that concern government entities or entities that receive government awards. For example, for engagements conducted in accordance with GAGAS, auditors may find it appropriate to use lower materiality levels than those used in non-GAGAS engagements because of the public accountability of government entities and entities receiving government funding, various legal and regulatory requirements, and the visibility and sensitivity of government programs.

Licensing and Certification

Requirements: Licensing and Certification

7.07 Auditors engaged to conduct examination engagements in the United States who do not work for a government audit organization should be licensed CPAs, persons working for licensed certified public accounting firms, or licensed accountants in states that have multiclass licensing systems that recognize licensed accountants other than CPAs.

7.08 Auditors engaged to conduct examination engagements of entities operating outside of the United States who do not work for a government audit organization should meet the qualifications indicated in paragraph 7.07, have certifications that meet all applicable national and international standards and serve in their respective countries as the functional equivalent of CPAs in the United States, or work for nongovernment audit organizations that are the functional equivalent of licensed certified public accounting firms in the United States.

Auditor Communication

Requirements: Auditor Communication

7.09 If the law or regulation requiring an examination engagement specifically identifies the entities to be examined, auditors should communicate pertinent information that in the auditors' professional judgment needs to be communicated both to individuals contracting for or requesting the examination and to those legislative committees, if any, that have ongoing oversight responsibilities for the audited entity.

7.10 If the identity of those charged with governance is not clearly evident, auditors should document the process followed and conclusions reached in identifying the appropriate individuals to receive the required communications.

Application Guidance: Auditor Communication

7.11 For some matters, early communication to those charged with governance or management may be important because of the relative significance and the urgency for corrective follow-up action. Further, early communication is important to allow management to take prompt corrective action to prevent further occurrences when a control deficiency results in identified or suspected noncompliance with provisions of laws, regulations, contracts, and grant agreements or identified or suspected fraud. When a deficiency is communicated early, the reporting requirements and application guidance in paragraphs 7.39 through 7.47 still apply.

7.12 Because the governance structures of government entities and organizations can vary widely, it may not always be clearly evident who is charged with key governance functions. The process for identifying those charged with governance includes evaluating the organizational structure for directing and controlling operations to achieve the audited entity's objectives and how the audited entity delegates authority and establishes accountability for management.

Results of Previous Engagements

Requirement: Results of Previous Engagements

7.13 When planning a GAGAS examination engagement, auditors should ask management of the audited entity to identify previous audits, attestation engagements, and other studies that directly relate to the subject matter or an assertion about the subject matter of the examination engagement, including whether related recommendations have been implemented. Auditors should evaluate whether the audited entity has taken appropriate corrective action to address findings and recommendations from previous engagements that could have a significant effect on the subject matter or an assertion about the subject matter. Auditors should use this information in assessing risk and determining the nature, timing, and extent of current work and determining the extent to which testing the implementation of the corrective actions is applicable to the current examination engagement objectives.

Investigations or Legal Proceedings

Requirement: Investigations or Legal Proceedings

7.14 Auditors should inquire of management of the audited entity whether any investigations or legal proceedings significant to the engagement objectives have been initiated or are in process with

Chapter 7: Standards for Attestation Engagements and Reviews of Financial Statements

respect to the period under examination, and should evaluate the effect of initiated or in-process investigations or legal proceedings on the current examination engagement.

Application Guidance: Investigations or Legal Proceedings

7.15 Laws, regulations, or policies may require auditors to report indications of certain types of fraud or noncompliance with provisions of laws, regulations, contracts, and grant agreements to law enforcement or investigatory authorities before performing additional examination procedures.

7.16 Avoiding interference with investigations or legal proceedings is important in pursuing indications of fraud and noncompliance with provisions of laws, regulations, contracts, and grant agreements. In some cases, it may be appropriate for the auditors to work with investigators or legal authorities or to withdraw from or defer further work on the attestation engagement or a portion of the engagement to avoid interfering with an ongoing investigation or legal proceeding.

Noncompliance with Provisions of Laws, Regulations, Contracts, and Grant Agreements

Requirement: Noncompliance with Provisions of Laws, Regulations, Contracts, and Grant Agreements

7.17 Auditors should extend the AICPA requirements concerning consideration of noncompliance with laws and regulations to include consideration of noncompliance with provisions of contracts and grant agreements.[52]

Application Guidance: Noncompliance with Provisions of Laws, Regulations, Contracts, and Grant Agreements

7.18 Government programs are subject to provisions of many laws, regulations, contracts, and grant agreements. At the same time, these provisions' significance within the context of the engagement objectives varies widely, depending on the objectives of the engagement. Auditors may consult with their legal counsel to (1) determine those laws and

---

[52]See paras. .32 and .33 of AT-C section 205 (AICPA, *Professional Standards*).

regulations that are significant to the examination objectives, (2) design tests of compliance with laws and regulations, and (3) evaluate the results of those tests. Auditors also may consult with their legal counsel when engagement objectives require testing compliance with provisions of contracts or grant agreements. Depending on the circumstances of the engagement, auditors may consult with others—such as investigative staff, other audit organizations or government entities that provided professional services to the audited entity, or applicable law enforcement authorities—to obtain information on compliance matters.

Findings

Requirements: Findings

7.19 When auditors identify findings, they should plan and perform procedures to develop the criteria, condition, cause, and effect of the findings to the extent that these elements are relevant and necessary to achieve the examination objectives.

7.20 Auditors should consider internal control deficiencies in their evaluation of identified findings when developing the cause element of the identified findings.

Application Guidance: Findings

7.21 Findings may involve deficiencies in internal control; noncompliance with provisions of laws, regulations, contracts, and grant agreements; or instances of fraud.

7.22 Given the concept of accountability for use of public resources and government authority, evaluating internal control in a government environment may also include considering internal control deficiencies that result in waste or abuse. Because the determination of waste and abuse is subjective, auditors are not required to perform specific procedures to detect waste or abuse in examinations. However, auditors may consider whether and how to communicate such matters if they become aware of them. Auditors may also discover that waste or abuse are indicative of fraud or noncompliance with provisions of laws, regulations, contracts, and grant agreements.

7.23 Waste is the act of using or expending resources carelessly, extravagantly, or to no purpose. Importantly, waste can include activities that do not include abuse and does not necessarily involve a violation of law. Rather, waste relates primarily to mismanagement, inappropriate actions, and inadequate oversight.

7.24 The following are examples of waste, depending on the facts and circumstances:

a. Making travel choices that are contrary to existing travel policies or are unnecessarily extravagant or expensive.

b. Making procurement or vendor selections that are contrary to existing policies or are unnecessarily extravagant or expensive.

7.25 Abuse is behavior that is deficient or improper when compared with behavior that a prudent person would consider reasonable and necessary business practice given the facts and circumstances, but excludes fraud and noncompliance with provisions of laws, regulations, contracts, and grant agreements. Abuse also includes misuse of authority or position for personal financial interests or those of an immediate or close family member or business associate.

7.26 The following are examples of abuse, depending on the facts and circumstances:

a. Creating unneeded overtime.

b. Requesting staff to perform personal errands or work tasks for a supervisor or manager.

c. Misusing the official's position for personal gain (including actions that could be perceived by an objective third party with knowledge of the relevant information as improperly benefiting an official's personal financial interests or those of an immediate or close family member; a general partner; an organization for which the official serves as an officer, director, trustee, or employee; or an organization with which the official is negotiating concerning future employment).

7.27 Criteria: For inclusion in findings, criteria may include the laws, regulations, contracts, grant agreements, standards, measures, expected performance, defined business practices, and benchmarks against which performance is compared or evaluated. Criteria identify the required or desired state or expectation with respect to the program or operation.

Chapter 7: Standards for Attestation Engagements and Reviews of Financial Statements

Criteria provide a context for evaluating evidence and understanding the findings, conclusions, and recommendations in the report.

7.28 Condition: Condition is a situation that exists. The condition is determined and documented during the attestation engagement.

7.29 Cause: The cause is the factor or factors responsible for the difference between the condition and the criteria, and may also serve as a basis for recommendations for corrective actions. Common factors include poorly designed policies, procedures, or criteria; inconsistent, incomplete, or incorrect implementation; or factors beyond the control of program management. Auditors may assess whether the evidence provides a reasonable and convincing argument for why the stated cause is the key factor contributing to the difference between the condition and the criteria.

7.30 Effect or potential effect: The effect or potential effect is the outcome or consequence resulting from the difference between the condition and the criteria. When the engagement objectives include identifying the actual or potential consequences of a condition that varies (either positively or negatively) from the criteria identified in the engagement, effect is a measure of those consequences. Effect or potential effect may be used to demonstrate the need for corrective action in response to identified problems or relevant risks.

7.31 Regardless of the type of finding identified, the cause of a finding may relate to an underlying internal control deficiency. Depending on the magnitude of impact, likelihood of occurrence, and nature of the deficiency, this deficiency could be a significant deficiency or a material weakness.

7.32 Considering internal control in the context of a comprehensive internal control framework, such as *Standards for Internal Control in the Federal Government* or *Internal Control—Integrated Framework*,[53] can

---

[53]The Committee of Sponsoring Organizations of the Treadway Commission's *Internal Control—Integrated Framework* and *Standards for Internal Control in the Federal Government* (GAO-14-704G) provide suitable and available criteria against which management may evaluate and report on the effectiveness of the entity's internal control. *Standards for Internal Control in the Federal Government* may be adopted by entities beyond those federal entities for which it is legally required, such as state, local, and quasi-governmental entities, as well as other federal entities and not-for-profit organizations, as a framework for an internal control system.

help auditors to determine whether underlying internal control deficiencies exist as the root cause of findings. Identifying these deficiencies can help provide the basis for developing meaningful recommendations for corrective actions.

Examination Engagement Documentation

Requirements: Examination Engagement Documentation

7.33 Auditors should comply with the following documentation requirements.

a. Before the date of the examination report, document supervisory review of the evidence that supports the findings, conclusions, and recommendations contained in the examination report.

b. Document any departures from the GAGAS requirements and the effect on the examination engagement and on the auditors' conclusions when the examination engagement does not comply with applicable GAGAS requirements because of law, regulation, scope limitations, restrictions on access to records, or other issues affecting the examination engagement.

7.34 In addition to the requirements of the examination engagement standards used in conjunction with GAGAS, auditors should prepare attest documentation in sufficient detail to enable an experienced auditor, having no previous connection to the examination engagement, to understand from the documentation the nature, timing, extent, and results of procedures performed and the evidence obtained and its source and the conclusions reached, including evidence that supports the auditors' significant judgments and conclusions.

Application Guidance: Examination Engagement Documentation

7.35 When documenting departures from the GAGAS requirements where alternative procedures performed were not sufficient to achieve the objectives of the requirements, the examination engagement documentation requirements apply to departures from unconditional requirements and presumptively mandatory requirements.

7.36 An experienced auditor is an individual who possesses the competencies and skills to be able to conduct the examination

Chapter 7: Standards for Attestation Engagements and Reviews of Financial Statements

engagement. These competencies and skills include an understanding of (1) examination engagement processes and related examination standards, (2) GAGAS and applicable legal and regulatory requirements, (3) the subject matter on which the auditors are engaged to report, (4) the suitability and availability of criteria, and (5) issues related to the audited entity's environment.

Availability of Individuals and Documentation

Requirement: Availability of Individuals and Documentation

7.37 Subject to applicable provisions of laws and regulations, auditors should make appropriate individuals and examination engagement documentation available upon request and in a timely manner to other auditors or reviewers.

Application Guidance: Availability of Individuals and Documentation

7.38 Underlying GAGAS examination engagements is the premise that audit organizations in federal, state, and local governments and public accounting firms engaged to conduct examination engagements in accordance with GAGAS cooperate in evaluating programs of common interest so that auditors may use others' work and avoid duplication of efforts. The use of auditors' work by other auditors may be facilitated by contractual arrangements for GAGAS engagements that provide for full and timely access to appropriate individuals and to engagement documentation.

Reporting the Auditors' Compliance with GAGAS

Requirements: Reporting the Auditors' Compliance with GAGAS

7.39 When auditors comply with all applicable GAGAS requirements, they should include a statement in the report that they conducted the examination in accordance with GAGAS.[54]

7.40 If auditors report separately (including separate reports bound in the same document) on deficiencies in internal control; noncompliance with provisions of laws, regulations, contracts, and grant agreements;

---

[54]See paras. 2.16 through 2.19 for information on the GAGAS compliance statement.

or instances of fraud, they should state in the examination report that they are issuing those additional reports. They should include a reference to the separate reports and also state that the reports are an integral part of a GAGAS examination engagement.

Application Guidance: Reporting the Auditors' Compliance with GAGAS

7.41 Because GAGAS incorporates by reference the AICPA's attestation standards, GAGAS does not require auditors to cite compliance with the AICPA standards when citing compliance with GAGAS. GAGAS does not prohibit auditors from issuing a separate report conforming only to the requirements of the AICPA or other standards.

Reporting Deficiencies in Internal Control

Requirement: Reporting Deficiencies in Internal Control

7.42 Auditors should include in the examination report all internal control deficiencies, even those communicated early, that are considered to be significant deficiencies or material weaknesses that the auditors identified based on the engagement work performed.[55]

Application Guidance: Reporting Deficiencies in Internal Control

7.43 Determining whether and how to communicate to officials of the audited entity internal control deficiencies that are not considered significant deficiencies or material weaknesses is a matter of professional judgment.

---

[55]GAGAS's use of internal control terminology is consistent with the definitions contained in AU-C section 265 (AICPA, *Professional Standards*).

Reporting on Noncompliance with Provisions of Laws, Regulations, Contracts, and Grant Agreements or Instances of Fraud

> **Requirements: Reporting on Noncompliance with Provisions of Laws, Regulations, Contracts, and Grant Agreements or Instances of Fraud**
>
> **7.44** Auditors should include in their examination report the relevant information about noncompliance and fraud when auditors, based on sufficient, appropriate evidence, identify or suspect
>
> a. noncompliance with provisions of laws, regulations, contracts, or grant agreements that has a material effect on the subject matter or an assertion about the subject matter or
>
> b. fraud that is material, either quantitatively or qualitatively, to the subject matter or an assertion about the subject matter that is significant to the engagement objectives.
>
> **7.45** When auditors identify or suspect noncompliance with provisions of laws, regulations, contracts, or grant agreements or instances of fraud that have an effect on the subject matter or an assertion about the subject matter that are less than material but warrant the attention of those charged with governance, they should communicate in writing to audited entity officials.

Application Guidance: Reporting on Noncompliance with Provisions of Laws, Regulations, Contracts, or Grant Agreements or Instances of Fraud

7.46 When auditors identify or suspect noncompliance with provisions of laws, regulations, contracts, or grant agreements or instances of fraud that do not warrant the attention of those charged with governance, the auditors' determination of whether and how to communicate such instances to audited entity officials is a matter of professional judgment.

7.47 When auditors identify or suspect noncompliance with provisions of laws, regulations, contracts, or grant agreements or instances of fraud, auditors may consult with authorities or legal counsel about whether publicly reporting such information would compromise investigative or legal proceedings. Auditors may limit their public reporting to matters that would not compromise those proceedings and, for example, report only on information that is already a part of the public record.

Presenting Findings in the Report

Requirements: Presenting Findings in the Report

7.48 When presenting findings, auditors should develop the elements of the findings to the extent necessary to assist management or oversight officials of the audited entity in understanding the need for taking corrective action.

7.49 Auditors should place their findings in perspective by describing the nature and extent of the issues being reported and the extent of the work performed that resulted in the findings. To give the reader a basis for judging the prevalence and consequences of the findings, auditors should, as appropriate, relate the instances identified to the population or the number of cases examined and quantify the results in terms of dollar value or other measures. If the results cannot be projected, auditors should limit their conclusions appropriately.

Application Guidance: Presenting Findings in the Report

7.50 Along with assisting management or oversight officials of the audited entity in understanding the need for taking corrective action, clearly developed findings assist auditors in making recommendations for corrective action. If auditors sufficiently develop the elements of a finding, they may provide recommendations for corrective action.

Reporting Findings Directly to Parties outside the Audited Entity

Requirements: Reporting Findings Directly to Parties outside the Audited Entity

7.51 Auditors should report identified or suspected noncompliance with provisions of laws, regulations, contracts, and grant agreements and instances of fraud directly to parties outside the audited entity in the following two circumstances.

a. When audited entity management fails to satisfy legal or regulatory requirements to report such information to external parties specified in law or regulation, auditors should first communicate the failure to report such information to those charged with governance. If the audited entity still does not report this information to the specified external parties as soon as practicable after the auditors' communication with those charged with governance, then the auditors should report the information directly to the specified external parties.

b. When audited entity management fails to take timely and appropriate steps to respond to fraud or noncompliance with provisions of laws, regulations, contracts, and grant agreements that (1) is likely to have a material effect on the subject matter and (2) involves funding received directly or indirectly from a government agency, auditors should first report management's failure to take timely and appropriate steps to those charged with governance. If the audited entity still does not take timely and appropriate steps as soon as practicable after the auditors' communication with those charged with governance, then the auditors should report the audited entity's failure to take timely and appropriate steps directly to the funding agency.

7.52 Auditors should comply with the requirements in paragraph 7.51 even if they have resigned or been dismissed from the engagement prior to its completion.

7.53 Auditors should obtain sufficient, appropriate evidence, such as confirmation from outside parties, to corroborate representations by management of the audited entity that it has reported engagement findings in accordance with laws, regulations, or funding agreements. When auditors are unable to do so, they should report such information directly, as discussed in paragraphs 7.51 and 7.52.

Application Guidance: Reporting Findings Directly to Parties outside the Audited Entity

7.54 The reporting in paragraph 7.51 is in addition to any legal requirements to report such information directly to parties outside the audited entity.

Obtaining and Reporting the Views of Responsible Officials

Requirements: Obtaining and Reporting the Views of Responsible Officials

7.55 Auditors should obtain and report the views of responsible officials of the audited entity concerning the findings, conclusions, and recommendations in the examination report, as well as any planned corrective actions.

7.56 When auditors receive written comments from the responsible officials, they should include in their report a copy of the officials' written comments or a summary of the comments received. When the responsible officials provide oral comments only, auditors should prepare a summary of the oral comments, provide a copy of the summary to the responsible officials to verify that the comments are accurately represented, and include the summary in their report.

7.57 When the audited entity's comments are inconsistent or in conflict with the findings, conclusions, or recommendations in the draft report, the auditors should evaluate the validity of the audited entity's comments. If the auditors disagree with the comments, they should explain in the report their reasons for disagreement. Conversely, the auditors should modify their report as necessary if they find the comments valid and supported by sufficient, appropriate evidence.

7.58 If the audited entity refuses to provide comments or is unable to provide comments within a reasonable period of time, the auditors should issue the report without receiving comments from the audited entity. In such cases, the auditors should indicate in the report that the audited entity did not provide comments.

Application Guidance: Obtaining and Reporting the Views of Responsible Officials

7.59 Providing a draft report with findings for review and comment by responsible officials of the audited entity and others helps the auditors develop a report that is fair, complete, and objective. Including the views of responsible officials results in a report that presents not only the auditors' findings, conclusions, and recommendations but also the perspectives of the audited entity's responsible officials and the corrective actions they plan to take. Obtaining the comments in writing is preferred, but oral comments are acceptable. When the audited entity provides technical comments in addition to its written or oral comments on the report, auditors may disclose in the report that such comments were received. Technical comments address points of fact or are editorial in nature and do not address substantive issues, such as methodology, findings, conclusions, or recommendations.

7.60 Obtaining oral comments may be appropriate when, for example, there is a reporting date critical to meeting a user's needs; auditors have worked closely with the responsible officials throughout the engagement, and the parties are familiar with the findings and issues addressed in the draft report; or the auditors do not expect major disagreements with findings, conclusions, or recommendations in the draft report or major controversies with regard to the issues discussed in the draft report.

Reporting Confidential or Sensitive Information

Requirements: Reporting Confidential or Sensitive Information

7.61 If certain information is prohibited from public disclosure or is excluded from a report because of its confidential or sensitive nature, auditors should disclose in the report that certain information has been omitted and the circumstances that make the omission necessary.

7.62 When circumstances call for omission of certain information, auditors should evaluate whether the omission could distort the examination engagement results or conceal improper or illegal practices and revise the report language as necessary to avoid report users drawing inappropriate conclusions from the information presented.

7.63 When the audit organization is subject to public records laws, auditors should determine whether public records laws could affect the availability of classified or limited use reports and determine whether other means of communicating with management and those charged with governance would be more appropriate. Auditors use professional judgment to determine the appropriate means to communicate the omitted information to management and those charged with governance considering, among other things, whether public records laws could affect the availability of classified or limited use reports.

Application Guidance: Reporting Confidential or Sensitive Information

7.64 If the report refers to the omitted information, the reference may be general and not specific. If the omitted information is not necessary to meet the engagement objectives, the report need not refer to its omission.

7.65 Certain information may be classified or may otherwise be prohibited from general disclosure by federal, state, or local laws or regulations. In such circumstances, auditors may issue a separate, classified, or limited use report containing such information and distribute the report only to persons authorized by law or regulation to receive it.

7.66 Additional circumstances associated with public safety, privacy, or security concerns could also justify the exclusion of certain information from a publicly available or widely distributed report. For example, detailed information related to computer security for a particular program may be excluded from publicly available reports because of the potential damage that misuse of this information could cause. In such circumstances, auditors may issue a limited use report containing such information and distribute the report only to those parties responsible for acting on the auditors' recommendations. In some instances, it may be appropriate to issue both a publicly available report with the sensitive information excluded and a limited use report. The auditors may consult with legal counsel regarding any requirements or other circumstances that may necessitate omitting certain information.

7.67 Considering the broad public interest in the program or activity under examination assists auditors when deciding whether to exclude certain information from publicly available reports.

7.68 In cases described in paragraph 7.63, the auditors may communicate general information in a written report and communicate detailed information orally. The auditors may consult with legal counsel regarding applicable public records laws.

Distributing Reports

Requirement: Distributing Reports

7.69 Distribution of reports completed in accordance with GAGAS depends on the auditors' relationship with the audited organization and the nature of the information contained in the reports. Auditors should document any limitation on report distribution.

   a. An audit organization in a government entity should distribute reports to those charged with governance, to the appropriate audited entity officials, and to the appropriate oversight bodies or organizations requiring or arranging for the examination engagements. As appropriate, auditors should also distribute copies of the reports to other officials who have legal oversight

Chapter 7: Standards for Attestation Engagements and Reviews of Financial Statements

authority or who may be responsible for acting on engagement findings and recommendations and to others authorized to receive such reports.

b. A public accounting firm contracted to conduct an examination engagement in accordance with GAGAS should clarify report distribution responsibilities with the engaging party. If the contracting firm is responsible for the distribution, it should reach agreement with the party contracting for the examination engagement about which officials or organizations will receive the report and the steps being taken to make the report available to the public.

Review Engagements

Compliance with Standards

Requirement: Compliance with Standards

7.70 GAGAS establishes requirements for review engagements in addition to the requirements for reviews contained in the AICPA's SSAEs. Auditors should comply with the additional GAGAS requirements, along with the applicable AICPA requirements, when citing GAGAS in their review engagement reports.

Licensing and Certification

Requirements: Licensing and Certification

7.71 Auditors engaged to conduct review engagements in the United States who do not work for a government audit organization should be licensed CPAs, persons working for licensed certified public accounting firms, or licensed accountants in states that have multiclass licensing systems that recognize licensed accountants other than CPAs.

7.72 Auditors engaged to conduct review engagements of entities operating outside of the United States who do not work for a

Chapter 7: Standards for Attestation Engagements and Reviews of Financial Statements

government audit organization should meet the qualifications indicated in paragraph 7.71, have certifications that meet all applicable national and international standards and serve in their respective countries as the functional equivalent of CPAs in the United States, or work for nongovernment audit organizations that are the functional equivalent of licensed certified public accounting firms in the United States.

Noncompliance with Provisions of Laws, Regulations, Contracts, and Grant Agreements

Requirement: Noncompliance with Provisions of Laws, Regulations, Contracts, and Grant Agreements

7.73 Auditors should extend the AICPA requirements concerning consideration of noncompliance with laws and regulations to include consideration of noncompliance with provisions of contracts and grant agreements.[56]

Reporting Auditors' Compliance with GAGAS

Requirement: Reporting Auditors' Compliance with GAGAS

7.74 When auditors comply with all applicable requirements for a review engagement conducted in accordance with GAGAS, they should include a statement in the review report that they conducted the engagement in accordance with GAGAS.[57]

Application Guidance: Reporting Auditors' Compliance with GAGAS

7.75 Because GAGAS incorporates by reference the AICPA's attestation standards, GAGAS does not require auditors to cite compliance with the AICPA standards when they cite compliance with GAGAS. GAGAS does not prohibit auditors from issuing a separate report conforming only to the requirements of the AICPA or other standards setters.

---

[56] See paras. .23 and .24 of AT-C section 210 (AICPA, *Professional Standards*).

[57] See paras. 2.16 through 2.19 for information on the GAGAS compliance statement.

Chapter 7: Standards for Attestation Engagements and Reviews of Financial Statements

7.76 Because review engagements are substantially less in scope than audits and examination engagements, it is important to include all required reporting elements contained in the standards used in conjunction with GAGAS. For example, a required element of the review report under SSAEs is a statement that a review is substantially less in scope than an examination, the objective of which is to express an opinion on the subject matter, and accordingly, no such opinion is expressed.[58] Including only those elements that the reporting standards for review engagements require or permit helps ensure that auditors comply with the standards and that users of GAGAS reports have an understanding of the nature of the work performed and the results of the review engagement.

Distributing Reports

Requirement: Distributing Reports

7.77 Distribution of reports completed in accordance with GAGAS depends on the auditors' relationship with the audited organization and the nature of the information contained in the reports. If the subject matter or the assertion involves material that is classified or contains confidential or sensitive information, auditors should limit report distribution. Auditors should document any limitation on report distribution.

a. An audit organization in a government entity should distribute reports to those charged with governance, to the appropriate audited entity officials, and to the appropriate oversight bodies or organizations requiring or arranging for the engagements. As appropriate, auditors should also distribute copies of the reports to other officials who have legal oversight authority and to others authorized to receive such reports.

b. A public accounting firm contracted to conduct a review engagement in accordance with GAGAS should clarify report distribution responsibilities with the engaging party. If the contracting firm is responsible for the distribution, it should reach agreement with the party contracting for the engagement

---

[58]See para. .46(f)(iii) of AT-C section 210 (AICPA, *Professional Standards*).

about which officials or organizations will receive the report and the steps being taken to make the report available to the public.

Agreed-Upon Procedures Engagements

Compliance with Standards

Requirement: Compliance with Standards

7.78 GAGAS establishes requirements for agreed-upon procedures engagements in addition to the requirements for agreed-upon procedures engagements contained in the AICPA's SSAEs. Auditors should comply with the additional GAGAS requirements, along with the applicable AICPA requirements, when citing GAGAS in their agreed-upon procedures engagement reports.

Licensing and Certification

Requirements: Licensing and Certification

7.79 Auditors engaged to conduct agreed-upon procedures engagements in the United States who do not work for a government audit organization should be licensed CPAs, persons working for licensed certified public accounting firms, or licensed accountants in states that have multiclass licensing systems that recognize licensed accountants other than CPAs.

7.80 Auditors engaged to conduct agreed-upon procedures engagements of entities operating outside of the United States who do not work for a government audit organization should meet the qualifications indicated in paragraph 7.79, have certifications that meet all applicable national and international standards and serve in their respective countries as the functional equivalent of CPAs in the United States, or work for nongovernment audit organizations that are the functional equivalent of licensed certified public accounting firms in the United States.

Noncompliance with Provisions of Laws, Regulations, Contracts, and Grant Agreements

Requirement: Noncompliance with Provisions of Laws, Regulations, Contracts, and Grant Agreements

7.81 Auditors should extend the AICPA requirements concerning consideration of noncompliance with laws and regulations to include consideration of noncompliance with provisions of contracts and grant agreements.[59]

Reporting Auditors' Compliance with GAGAS

Requirement: Reporting Auditors' Compliance with GAGAS

7.82 When auditors comply with all applicable GAGAS requirements for agreed-upon procedures engagements, they should include a statement in the agreed-upon procedures engagement report that they conducted the engagement in accordance with GAGAS.[60]

Application Guidance: Reporting Auditors' Compliance with GAGAS

7.83 Because GAGAS incorporates by reference the AICPA's attestation standards, GAGAS does not require auditors to cite compliance with the AICPA standards when citing compliance with GAGAS. GAGAS does not prohibit auditors from issuing a separate report conforming only to the requirements of the AICPA or other standards.

7.84 Because agreed-upon procedures engagements are substantially less in scope than audits and examination engagements, it is important not to deviate from the required reporting elements contained in the attestation standards incorporated by reference in GAGAS, other than

---

[59]See para. .42 of AT-C section 215 (AICPA, *Professional Standards*).

[60]See paras. 2.16 through 2.19 for information on the GAGAS compliance statement.

Chapter 7: Standards for Attestation Engagements and Reviews of Financial Statements

including the reference to GAGAS. For example, a required element of the report on agreed-upon procedures is a statement that the auditors were not engaged to and did not conduct an examination or a review of the subject matter, the objective of which would be the expression of an opinion or a conclusion, respectively, and that had the auditors performed additional procedures, other matters may have come to their attention that would have been reported.[61] Another required element is a statement that the sufficiency of the procedures is solely the responsibility of the parties specified in the report and a disclaimer of responsibility for sufficiency of those procedures.[62] Including only those elements that the AICPA reporting standards for agreed-upon procedures engagements require or permit helps ensure that auditors comply with the AICPA standards and that users of GAGAS reports understand the nature of the work performed and the results of the agreed-upon procedures engagement.

Distributing Reports

Requirement: Distributing Reports

7.85 Distribution of reports completed in accordance with GAGAS depends on the auditors' relationship with the audited organization and the nature of the information contained in the reports. If the subject matter or the assertion involves material that is classified or contains confidential or sensitive information, auditors should limit the report distribution. Auditors should document any limitation on report distribution.

   a. An audit organization in a government entity should distribute reports to those charged with governance, to the appropriate audited entity officials, and to the appropriate oversight bodies or organizations requiring or arranging for the engagements. As appropriate, auditors should also distribute copies of the reports to other officials who have legal oversight authority and to others authorized to receive such reports.

   b. A public accounting firm contracted to conduct an agreed-upon procedures engagement in accordance with GAGAS should

---

[61]See para. .35(j) of AT-C section 215 (AICPA, *Professional Standards*).

[62]See para. .35(g) of AT-C section 215 (AICPA, *Professional Standards*).

> clarify report distribution responsibilities with the engaging party. If the contracting firm is responsible for the distribution, it should reach agreement with the party contracting for the engagement about which officials or organizations will receive the report and the steps being taken to make the report available to the public.

Reviews of Financial Statements

Compliance with Standards

Requirement: Compliance with Standards

7.86 GAGAS establishes requirements for reviews of financial statements in addition to the requirements for reviews of financial statements contained in the AICPA's AR-C section 90, *Review of Financial Statements*.[63] Auditors should comply with the additional GAGAS requirements, along with the applicable AICPA requirements, when citing GAGAS in their review engagement reports.

Licensing and Certification

Requirements: Licensing and Certification

7.87 Auditors engaged to conduct reviews of financial statements in the United States who do not work for a government audit organization should be licensed CPAs, persons working for licensed certified public accounting firms, or licensed accountants in states that have multiclass licensing systems that recognize licensed accountants other than CPAs.

7.88 Auditors engaged to conduct reviews of financial statements of entities operating outside of the United States who do not work for a government audit organization should meet the qualifications indicated

---

[63]AICPA, *Professional Standards*.

in paragraph 7.87, have certifications that meet all applicable national and international standards and serve in their respective countries as the functional equivalent of CPAs in the United States, or work for nongovernment audit organizations that are the functional equivalent of licensed certified public accounting firms in the United States.

Noncompliance with Provisions of Laws, Regulations, Contracts, and Grant Agreements

Requirement: Noncompliance with Provisions of Laws, Regulations, Contracts, and Grant Agreements

7.89 Auditors should extend the AICPA requirements concerning consideration of noncompliance with laws and regulations to include consideration of noncompliance with provisions of contracts and grant agreements.[64]

Reporting Auditors' Compliance with GAGAS

Requirement: Reporting Auditors' Compliance with GAGAS

7.90 When auditors comply with all applicable requirements for a review of financial statements conducted in accordance with GAGAS, they should include a statement in the report that they conducted the engagement in accordance with GAGAS.[65]

Application Guidance: Reporting Auditors' Compliance with GAGAS

7.91 Because GAGAS incorporates by reference the AICPA's AR-C section 90, *Review of Financial Statements*,[66] GAGAS does not require auditors to cite compliance with the AICPA standards when they cite compliance with GAGAS. GAGAS does not prohibit auditors from issuing a separate report conforming only to the requirements of the AICPA or other standards setters.

---

[64] See para. .51 of AR-C section 90 (AICPA, *Professional Standards*).

[65] See paras. 2.16 through 2.19 for information on the GAGAS compliance statement.

[66] AICPA, *Professional Standards*.

Chapter 7: Standards for Attestation Engagements and Reviews of Financial Statements

7.92 Because reviews of financial statements are substantially less in scope than audits and examination engagements, it is important to include all required reporting elements contained in the standards used in conjunction with GAGAS. For example, a required reporting element of the review of financial statements under AR-C section 90, *Review of Financial Statements*,[67] is to include a statement that a review is substantially less in scope than an audit, the objective of which is the expression of an opinion regarding the financial statements as a whole and that accordingly the accountant does not express such an opinion.[68] Including only those elements that the reporting standards for review of financial statements engagements require or permit helps ensure that auditors comply with the standards and that users of GAGAS reports have an understanding of the nature of the work performed and the results of the review engagement.

Distributing Reports

Requirement: Distributing Reports

7.93 Distribution of reports completed in accordance with GAGAS depends on the auditors' relationship with the audited organization and the nature of the information contained in the reports. If the subject matter involves material that is classified or contains confidential or sensitive information, auditors should limit report distribution. Auditors should document any limitation on report distribution.

a. An audit organization in a government entity should distribute reports to those charged with governance, to the appropriate audited entity officials, and to the appropriate oversight bodies or organizations requiring or arranging for the engagements. As appropriate, auditors should also distribute copies of the reports to other officials who have legal oversight authority and to others authorized to receive such reports.

b. A public accounting firm contracted to conduct a review of financial statements engagement in accordance with GAGAS should clarify report distribution responsibilities with the engaging party. If the contracting firm is responsible for the

---

[67]AICPA, *Professional Standards*.

[68]See para. .39(c)(vi) of AR-C section 90 (AICPA, *Professional Standards*).

distribution, it should reach agreement with the party contracting for the engagement about which officials or organizations will receive the report and the steps being taken to make the report available to the public.

Chapter 8: Fieldwork Standards for Performance Audits

8.01 This chapter contains fieldwork requirements and guidance for performance audits conducted in accordance with generally accepted government auditing standards (GAGAS). Fieldwork requirements establish an overall approach for auditors to apply in planning and performing an audit to obtain sufficient, appropriate evidence that provides a reasonable basis for findings and conclusions based on the audit objectives. For performance audits conducted in accordance with GAGAS, the requirements and guidance in chapters 1 through 5 and chapter 9 also apply.

8.02 The fieldwork requirements for performance audits relate to planning the audit; conducting the engagement; supervising staff; obtaining sufficient, appropriate evidence; and preparing audit documentation. The concepts of evidence, significance, and audit risk form a framework for applying these requirements and are included throughout the discussion of performance audits.

Planning

Requirements: General

8.03 Auditors must adequately plan the work necessary to address the audit objectives. Auditors must document the audit plan.

8.04 Auditors must plan the audit to reduce audit risk to an acceptably low level.

8.05 In planning the audit, auditors should assess significance and audit risk. Auditors should apply these assessments to establish the scope and methodology for addressing the audit objectives. Planning is a continuous process throughout the audit.

8.06 Auditors should design the methodology to obtain sufficient, appropriate evidence that provides a reasonable basis for findings and conclusions based on the audit objectives and to reduce audit risk to an acceptably low level.

8.07 Auditors should identify and use suitable criteria based on the audit objectives.

Application Guidance: General

8.08 The audit objectives are what the audit is intended to accomplish. They identify the audit subject matter and performance aspects to be included. Audit objectives can be thought of as questions about the program that the auditors seek to answer based on evidence obtained and assessed against criteria. Audit objectives may also pertain to the current status or condition of a program. The term program as used in GAGAS includes processes, projects, studies, policies, operations, activities, entities, and functions.

8.09 Auditors may need to refine or adjust the audit objectives, scope, and methodology as work is performed. However, in situations where the audit objectives are established by statute or legislative oversight, auditors may not have latitude to define or adjust the audit objectives or scope.

8.10 Scope is the boundary of the audit and is directly tied to the audit objectives. The scope defines the subject matter that the auditors will assess and report on, such as a particular program or aspect of a program, the necessary documents or records, the period of time reviewed, and the locations that will be included.

8.11 The methodology describes the nature and extent of audit procedures for gathering and analyzing evidence to address the audit objectives. Audit procedures are the specific steps and tests auditors perform to address the audit objectives.

8.12 Obtaining sufficient, appropriate evidence provides auditors with a reasonable basis for findings and conclusions that are valid, accurate, appropriate, and complete with respect to the audit objectives.

8.13 The sufficiency and appropriateness of evidence needed and tests of evidence are determined by the auditors based on the audit objectives, findings, and conclusions. Objectives for performance audits range from narrow to broad and involve varying types and quality of evidence. In some engagements, sufficient, appropriate evidence is available, but in others, information may have limitations. Professional judgment assists auditors in determining the audit scope and methodology needed to address the audit objectives and in evaluating whether sufficient, appropriate evidence has been obtained to address the audit objectives.

Chapter 8: Fieldwork Standards for
Performance Audits

8.14 In performance audits conducted in accordance with GAGAS, auditors are the party who measures or evaluates the subject matter of the engagement and who presents the resulting information as part of, or accompanying, the audit report. Therefore, GAGAS does not require auditors to obtain management assertions with respect to the subject matter when conducting a performance audit.

8.15 The concept of significance assists auditors throughout a performance audit, including when deciding the type and extent of audit work to perform, when evaluating results of audit work, and when developing the report and related findings and conclusions. Significance is defined as the relative importance of a matter within the context in which it is being considered, including quantitative and qualitative factors. Such factors include the magnitude of the matter in relation to the subject matter of the audit, the nature and effect of the matter, the relevance of the matter, the needs and interests of an objective third party with knowledge of the relevant information, and the matter's effect on the audited program or activity. Professional judgment assists auditors when evaluating the significance of matters within the context of the audit objectives. In the performance audit requirements, the term significant is comparable to the term material as used in the context of financial statement engagements.

8.16 Audit risk is the possibility that the auditors' findings, conclusions, recommendations, or assurance may be improper or incomplete as a result of factors such as evidence that is not sufficient or appropriate, an inadequate audit process, or intentional omissions or misleading information because of misrepresentation or fraud. The assessment of audit risk involves both qualitative and quantitative considerations. Factors affecting audit risk include the time frames, complexity, or sensitivity of the work; size of the program in terms of dollar amounts and number of citizens served; adequacy of the audited entity's systems and processes for preventing and detecting inconsistencies, significant errors, or fraud; and auditors' access to records. Audit risk includes the risk that auditors will not detect a mistake, inconsistency, significant error, or fraud in the evidence supporting the audit. Audit risk can be reduced by taking actions such as increasing the scope of work; adding specialists, additional reviewers, and other resources to conduct the audit; changing the methodology to obtain additional evidence, higher-quality evidence, or alternative forms of corroborating evidence; or aligning the findings and conclusions to reflect the evidence obtained.

8.17 Criteria identify the required or desired state or expectation with respect to the program or operation. Criteria provide a context for evaluating evidence and understanding the findings, conclusions, and recommendations in the report. Suitable criteria are relevant, reliable, objective, and understandable and do not result in the omission of significant information, as applicable, within the context of the audit objectives. The relative importance of each of these characteristics to a particular engagement is a matter of professional judgment. In instances where laws, regulations, or policies prescribe the criteria to be used for the engagement, such criteria are presumed to be suitable in the absence of indications to the contrary.

8.18 Examples of criteria include

   a. laws and regulations applicable to the operation of the audited entity;

   b. goals, policies, and procedures established by officials of the audited entity;

   c. technically developed standards or norms;

   d. expert opinions;

   e. prior periods' performance;

   f. defined business practices;

   g. contracts or grant agreements; and

   h. benchmarks against which performance is compared, including performance of other entities or sectors.

8.19 For audit objectives that pertain to the current status or condition of a program, sufficient, appropriate evidence is gathered to provide reasonable assurance that the description of the current status or condition of a program is accurate and reliable and does not omit significant information relevant to the audit objectives. Information addressing the audit objectives is to be provided in an objective, understandable manner. The relative importance of each of the characteristics of the information to a particular engagement is a matter of professional judgment.

Auditor Communication

Requirements: Auditor Communication

8.20 Auditors should communicate an overview of the objectives, scope, and methodology and the timing of the performance audit and planned reporting (including any potential restrictions on the report), unless doing so could significantly impair the auditors' ability to obtain sufficient, appropriate evidence to address the audit objectives. Auditors should communicate such information with the following parties, as applicable:

   a. management of the audited entity, including those with sufficient authority and responsibility to implement corrective action in the program or activity being audited;

   b. those charged with governance;

   c. the individuals contracting for or requesting audit services, such as contracting officials or grantees; or

   d. the cognizant legislative committee, when auditors conduct the audit pursuant to a law or regulation or when they conduct the work for the legislative committee that has oversight of the audited entity.

8.21 In situations where the parties required to receive communications, as described in paragraph 8.20, are not clearly evident, auditors should document the process followed and conclusions reached in identifying the appropriate individuals to receive the required communications.

8.22 Auditors should retain any written communication resulting from paragraph 8.20 as audit documentation.

Application Guidance: Auditor Communication

8.23 Determining the form, content, and frequency of the communication with management or those charged with governance is a matter of professional judgment, although written communication is preferred. Auditors may use an engagement letter to communicate key information early in the engagement.

8.24 Examples of communications regarding the objectives, scope, methodology, and timing that could impair the auditors' ability to obtain sufficient, appropriate evidence include situations in which the auditors plan to perform unannounced cash counts or perform procedures related to indications of fraud.

8.25 Communicating with those charged with governance or management may include communicating deficiencies in internal control; fraud; or noncompliance with provisions of laws, regulations, contracts, and grant agreements. Early communication of these matters may be important because of their relative significance and the urgency for corrective follow-up action. Further, early communication is important to allow management to take prompt corrective action to prevent further occurrences when a control deficiency results in noncompliance with provisions of laws, regulations, contracts, and grant agreements or fraud. When a deficiency is communicated early, the reporting requirements and application guidance in paragraphs 9.29 through 9.44 still apply.

8.26 Because the governance structures of government entities and organizations can vary widely, it may not always be clearly evident who is charged with key governance functions. The process for identifying those charged with governance includes evaluating the organizational structure for directing and controlling operations to achieve the audited entity's objectives and how the audited entity delegates authority and establishes accountability for management.

Investigations or Legal Proceedings

Requirement: Investigations or Legal Proceedings

8.27 Auditors should inquire of management of the audited entity whether any investigations or legal proceedings significant to the audit objectives have been initiated or are in process with respect to the period under audit, and should evaluate the effect of initiated or in-process investigations or legal proceedings on the current audit.

Application Guidance: Investigations or Legal Proceedings

8.28 Laws, regulations, or policies may require auditors to report indications of the following to law enforcement or investigatory authorities before performing additional audit procedures: certain types of fraud or noncompliance with provisions of laws, regulations, contracts, and grant agreements.

8.29 Avoiding interference with investigations or legal proceedings is important in pursuing indications of fraud and noncompliance with provisions of laws, regulations, contracts, and grant agreements. In some cases, it may be appropriate for the auditors to work with investigators or legal authorities or to withdraw from or defer further work on the engagement or a portion of the engagement to avoid interfering with an ongoing investigation or legal proceeding.

Results of Previous Engagements

Requirement: Results of Previous Engagements

8.30 Auditors should evaluate whether the audited entity has taken appropriate corrective action to address findings and recommendations from previous engagements that are significant within the context of the audit objectives. When planning the audit, auditors should ask management of the audited entity to identify previous engagements or other studies that directly relate to the objectives of the audit, including whether related recommendations have been implemented. Auditors should use this information in assessing risk and determining the nature, timing, and extent of current audit work, including determining the extent to which testing the implementation of the corrective actions is applicable to the current audit objectives.

Assigning Auditors

Requirements: Assigning Auditors

8.31 Audit management should assign sufficient auditors with adequate collective professional competence, as described in paragraphs 4.02 through 4.15, to conduct the audit. Staffing an audit includes, among other things,

  a. assigning auditors with the collective knowledge, skills, and abilities appropriate for the audit;

  b. assigning a sufficient number of auditors to the audit;

  c. providing for on-the-job training of auditors; and

d. engaging specialists when necessary.

8.32 If planning to use the work of specialists, auditors should document the nature and scope of the work to be performed by the specialists, including

a. the objectives and scope of the specialists' work,

b. the intended use of the specialists' work to support the audit objectives,

c. the specialists' procedures and findings so they can be evaluated and related to other planned audit procedures, and

d. the assumptions and methods used by the specialists.

Preparing a Written Audit Plan

Requirement: Preparing a Written Audit Plan

8.33 Auditors must prepare a written audit plan for each audit. Auditors should update the plan, as necessary, to reflect any significant changes to the plan made during the audit.

Application Guidance: Preparing a Written Audit Plan

8.34 The form and content of the written audit plan may vary among audits and may include an audit strategy, audit program, project plan, audit planning paper, or other appropriate documentation of key decisions about the audit objectives, scope, and methodology and the auditors' basis for those decisions.

8.35 A written audit plan provides an opportunity for audit organization management to supervise audit planning and to determine whether

a. the proposed audit objectives are likely to result in a useful report;

b. the audit plan adequately addresses relevant risks;

c. the proposed audit scope and methodology are adequate to address the audit objectives;

d. available evidence is likely to be sufficient and appropriate for purposes of the audit; and

e. sufficient staff, supervisors, and specialists with adequate collective professional competence and other resources are available to conduct the audit and to meet expected time frames for completing the work.

Conducting the Engagement

Nature and Profile of the Program and User Needs

Requirement: Nature and Profile of the Program and User Needs

8.36 Auditors should obtain an understanding of the nature of the program or program component under audit and the potential use that will be made of the audit results or report as they plan a performance audit. The nature and profile of a program include

a. visibility, sensitivity, and relevant risks associated with the program under audit;

b. age of the program or changes in its condition;

c. the size of the program in terms of total dollars, number of citizens affected, or other measures;

d. level and extent of review or other forms of independent oversight;

e. the program's strategic plan and objectives; and

f. external factors or conditions that could directly affect the program.

Application Guidance: Nature and Profile of the Program and User Needs

8.37 One group of users of the audit report is government officials or other parties who authorize or request audits. Other important users of the audit report are the audited entity, those responsible for acting on the auditors' recommendations, oversight organizations, and legislative bodies. Other potential users of the audit report include legislators or government officials (other than those who authorized or requested the audit), the media, interest groups, and individual citizens. In addition to an interest in the program, potential users may have an ability to influence the conduct of the program. An awareness of these potential users' interests and influence can help auditors judge whether possible findings could be significant to relevant users.

8.38 Obtaining an understanding of the program under audit helps auditors to assess the relevant risks associated with the program and the effect of the risks on the audit objectives, scope, and methodology. The auditors' understanding may come from knowledge they already have about the program or knowledge they gain from inquiries, observations, and reviewing documents while planning the audit. The extent and breadth of those inquiries and observations will vary among audits based on the audit objectives, as will the need to understand individual aspects of the program, such as the following:

   a. Provisions of laws, regulations, contracts, and grant agreements: Government programs are usually created by law and are subject to specific laws and regulations. Laws and regulations usually set forth what is to be done, who is to do it, the purpose to be achieved, the population to be served, and related funding guidelines or restrictions. Government programs may also be subject to contracts or grant agreements. Thus, understanding the laws and legislative history establishing a program and the provisions of contracts or grant agreements is essential to understanding the program itself. Obtaining that understanding is also a necessary step in identifying the provisions of laws, regulations, contracts, and grant agreements that are significant within the context of the audit objectives.

   b. Purpose and goals: Purpose is the result or effect that is intended or desired from a program's operation. Legislatures usually establish a program's purpose when they provide authority for the program. Audited entity officials may provide more detailed information on the program's purpose to supplement the authorizing legislation. Audited entity officials are sometimes asked to set goals for program performance and operations, including both output and outcome goals. Auditors may use the stated program purpose and goals as criteria for assessing program performance or may develop additional criteria to use when assessing performance.

c. Internal control: Internal control is a process effected by an entity's oversight body, management, and other personnel that provides reasonable assurance that the objectives of an entity will be achieved. Internal control comprises the plans, methods, policies, and procedures used to fulfill the mission, strategic plan, goals, and objectives of the entity.

d. Inputs: Inputs are the amount of resources (in terms of, for example, money, material, or personnel) that is put into a program. These resources may come from within or outside the entity operating the program. Measures of inputs can have a number of dimensions, such as cost, timing, and quality. Examples of measures of inputs are dollars spent, employee hours expended, and square feet of building space used.

e. Program operations: Program operations are the strategies, processes, and activities management uses to convert inputs into outputs. Program operations may be subject to internal control.

f. Outputs: Outputs represent the quantity of goods or services produced by a program. For example, an output measure for a job training program could be the number of persons completing training, and an output measure for an aviation safety inspection program could be the number of safety inspections completed.

g. Outcomes: Outcomes are accomplishments or results of a program. For example, an outcome measure for a job training program could be the percentage of trained persons obtaining a job and still in the workplace after a specified period. An example of an outcome measure for an aviation safety inspection program could be the percentage reduction in safety problems found in subsequent inspections or the percentage of problems deemed corrected in follow-up inspections. Such outcome measures show the progress made in achieving the stated program purposes of helping unemployed citizens obtain and retain jobs and improving

Chapter 8: Fieldwork Standards for
Performance Audits

the safety of aviation operations, respectively. Outcomes may be influenced by cultural, economic, physical, or technological factors outside the program. Auditors may use approaches drawn from other disciplines, such as program evaluation, to isolate the effects of the program from these other influences. Outcomes also include a program's unexpected or unintentional effects, both positive and negative.

Determining Significance and Obtaining an Understanding of Internal Control

Requirements: Determining Significance and Obtaining an Understanding of Internal Control

8.39 Auditors should determine and document whether internal control is significant to the audit objectives.[69]

8.40 If it is determined that internal control is significant to the audit objectives, auditors should obtain an understanding of such internal control.

Application Guidance: Determining Significance and Obtaining an Understanding of Internal Control

8.41 Consideration of internal control in a performance audit begins with determining the significance of internal control to the audit objectives and documenting that determination. Some factors that may be considered when determining the significance of internal control to the audit objectives include

a. the subject matter under audit, such as the program or program component under audit, including the audited entity's objectives for the program and associated inherent risks;

b. the nature of findings and conclusions expected to be reported, based on the needs and interests of audit report users;

---

[69]See fig.4 at the end of ch. 8 for a flowchart on consideration of internal control in a GAGAS performance audit.

c. the three categories of entity objectives (operations, reporting, and compliance);[70] and

d. the five components of internal control (control environment, risk assessment, control activities, information and communication, and monitoring) and the integration of the components.

8.42 If internal control is significant to the audit objectives, auditors determine which of the five components of internal control and underlying principles are significant to the audit objectives, as all components of internal control are generally relevant, but not all components may be significant to the audit objectives. This determination can also identify whether specific controls are significant to the audit objectives. Determining which internal control components and principles and/or specific controls are significant to the audit objectives is a matter of professional judgment.

8.43 Determining the significance of internal control may be an iterative process. As discussed in paragraph 8.09, the audit objectives can evolve and become more refined throughout the audit. When this occurs, the significance of internal control is determined and documented for the new or revised objectives.

8.44 Determining the significance of internal control may be documented in formats such as narratives or tables. The documentation includes the conclusions on whether internal control is significant to the audit objectives, and if so, which components of internal control are significant to the audit objectives. The documentation may also include the factors considered and steps taken to perform the determination.

8.45 Determining the significance of internal control to the audit objectives affects the audit planning required in paragraphs 8.03 through 8.07. Specifically, it enables auditors to determine whether to assess internal control as part of the audit and, if they do, to identify criteria for the assessment and plan the appropriate scope, methodology, and extent of internal control assessments to perform.

---

[70]The terminology used in this section is consistent with the definitions and concepts in the Committee of Sponsoring Organizations of the Treadway Commission's *Internal Control—Integrated Framework* (COSO Framework) and *Standards for Internal Control in the Federal Government* (GAO-14-704G) (Green Book).

Chapter 8: Fieldwork Standards for Performance Audits

8.46 The nature and extent of procedures auditors perform to obtain an understanding of internal control is a matter of professional judgment and may vary among audits based on audit objectives, audit risk, internal control deficiencies, and the auditors' knowledge about internal control gained in prior audits. The understanding of internal control builds on the understanding of the program required in paragraph 8.36. The auditors' understanding of internal control may be obtained through procedures such as inquiries, observations, inspection of documents and records, review of other audit reports, or direct tests.

8.47 Approaches for obtaining an understanding of internal control may vary and may include consideration of entity-level controls, transaction-level controls, or both. However, even when assessing only transaction-level controls, it may be beneficial to gain an understanding of entity-level controls that may affect transaction-level controls by obtaining a broad understanding of the five components of internal control at the entity level. This involves considering the relationships between the components, which work together in an integrated manner in an effective internal control system, and the principles of internal control that support each component. In addition to obtaining a broad understanding of internal control at the entity level, auditors may also obtain an understanding of internal control at the transaction level for the specific programs and processes under audit.

8.48 Obtaining an understanding of internal control assists auditors in identifying an audited entity's key controls relevant to the audit objectives. Identifying key controls involves considering the entity's objectives that are relevant to the audit and whether the entity has controls in place to achieve those objectives and address associated risks. Collectively, key controls are those controls necessary to achieve the entity's control objectives and provide reasonable assurance of achieving the entity's objectives. Key controls often have one or both of the following characteristics:

　　a. Their failure may significantly affect the achievement of the entity's objectives, yet not reasonably be detected in a timely manner by other controls.

　　b. Their operation may prevent or detect other control failures before they have an opportunity to become significant to the achievement of the entity's objectives.

Assessing Internal Control

Requirement: Assessing Internal Control

8.49 If internal control is determined to be significant to the audit objectives, auditors should assess and document their assessment of the design, implementation, and/or operating effectiveness of such internal control to the extent necessary to address the audit objectives.

Application Guidance: Assessing Internal Control

8.50 The auditors' understanding of internal control provides a basis for determining the nature, timing, and extent of procedures for assessments of internal control, if such an assessment will be performed. Assessments of internal control in a performance audit are performed to the extent necessary to address the audit objectives. The levels of internal control assessment that may be performed based on the audit objectives are (1) assessing the design; (2) assessing the design and implementation; or (3) assessing the design, implementation, and operating effectiveness of controls that are significant to the audit objectives.

8.51 Assessments of internal control involve designing and performing procedures to obtain sufficient, appropriate evidence, as required in paragraphs 8.90 through 8.94, to support and document the auditors' findings and conclusions on design, implementation, and/or operating effectiveness of controls that are significant to the audit objectives. The controls being assessed are generally the key controls identified during the planning phase of the engagement, which may include controls at both the entity and transaction levels. Changes may be made to the initial determination of key controls based on additional information gathered during the course of fieldwork.

8.52 The design of internal control is assessed by determining whether controls individually and in combination are capable of achieving an objective and addressing the related risk. The implementation of internal control is assessed by determining if the control exists and has been placed into operation. The operating effectiveness of internal control is assessed by determining whether controls were applied at relevant times during the period under evaluation, the consistency with which they were applied, and by whom or by what means they were applied. A control cannot be effectively implemented if it was not effectively designed. A control cannot be operating effectively if it was not effectively designed and implemented.

Chapter 8: Fieldwork Standards for
Performance Audits

8.53 During the assessment of each control, deficiencies in internal control may be identified. A deficiency in internal control exists when the design, implementation, or operation of a control does not allow management or personnel to achieve control objectives and address related risks.[71] A deficiency in design exists when a necessary control is missing or is not properly designed so that even if the control operates as designed, the control objective would not be met. A deficiency in implementation exists when a control is properly designed but not implemented correctly in the internal control system. A deficiency in operating effectiveness exists when a properly designed control does not operate as designed or the person performing the control does not have the necessary competence or authority to perform the control effectively.

Internal Control Deficiencies Considerations

Requirement: Internal Control Deficiencies Considerations

8.54 Auditors should evaluate and document the significance of identified internal control deficiencies within the context of the audit objectives.

Application Guidance: Internal Control Deficiencies Considerations

8.55 Internal control deficiencies are evaluated for significance within the context of the audit objectives. Deficiencies are evaluated both on an individual basis and in the aggregate. Consideration is given to the correlation among deficiencies. This evaluation and the audit work performed form the basis of the auditors' determination whether, individually or in combination, the deficiencies are significant within the context of the audit objectives.[72]

8.56 Determining whether deficiencies are significant within the context of the audit objectives involves evaluating the following factors:

　　a. Magnitude of impact: Magnitude of impact refers to the likely effect that the deficiency could have on the entity achieving its objectives and is affected by factors such as the size, pace, and duration of

---

[71]See paras. 1.27g and 1.27k for definitions of control objective and entity objective.

[72]See paras. 9.29 through 9.34 for a discussion of reporting on internal control.

the deficiency's impact. A deficiency may be more significant to one objective than another.

b. Likelihood of occurrence: Likelihood of occurrence refers to the possibility of a deficiency impacting an entity's ability to achieve its objectives.

c. Nature of the deficiency: The nature of the deficiency involves factors such as the degree of subjectivity involved with the deficiency and whether the deficiency arises from fraud or misconduct.

8.57 Internal control deficiencies are a type of finding, and the requirements related to developing the four elements of a finding in paragraph 8.116 apply. When determining the cause of internal control deficiencies, it may be helpful for auditors to perform an analysis to identify the root cause of the deficiencies. Identifying the root causes of internal control deficiencies may strengthen the quality of auditors' recommendations for corrective actions.

8.58 The following are examples of control deficiencies:

a. Ineffective oversight by those charged with governance of the entity's financial reporting, performance reporting, or internal control, or an ineffective overall governance structure.

b. An ineffective internal audit function or risk assessment function at an entity for which such functions are important to the monitoring or risk assessment component of internal control, such as for a large or complex entity.

c. Failure by management or those charged with governance to assess the effect of a deficiency previously communicated to them and either to correct it or to conclude that it does not need to be corrected.

d. Inadequate controls for the safeguarding of assets.

e. Inadequate design of information systems general, application, and user controls that prevents an information system from providing complete and accurate information consistent with financial, compliance, or performance reporting objectives or other current needs.

f. Failure of an application control caused by a deficiency in the design or operation of an information system's general controls.

g. Employees or management who lack the qualifications and training to fulfill their assigned functions.

Information Systems Controls Considerations

Requirements: Information Systems Controls Considerations

8.59 The effectiveness of significant internal controls frequently depends on the effectiveness of information systems controls. Thus, when obtaining an understanding of internal control significant to the audit objectives, auditors should also determine whether it is necessary to evaluate information systems controls.

8.60 When information systems controls are determined to be significant to the audit objectives or when the effectiveness of significant controls depends on the effectiveness of information systems controls, auditors should then evaluate the design, implementation, and/or operating effectiveness of such controls. This evaluation includes other information systems controls that affect the effectiveness of the significant controls or the reliability of information used in performing the significant controls. Auditors should obtain a sufficient understanding of information systems controls necessary to assess audit risk and plan the audit within the context of the audit objectives.

8.61 Auditors should determine which audit procedures related to information systems controls are needed to obtain sufficient, appropriate evidence to support the audit findings and conclusions.

8.62 When evaluating information systems controls is an audit objective, auditors should test information systems controls to the extent necessary to address the audit objective.

Application Guidance: Information Systems Controls Considerations

8.63 Understanding information systems controls is important when information systems are used extensively throughout the program under audit and the fundamental business processes related to the audit objectives rely on information systems. Information systems controls consist of those internal controls that depend on information systems processing and include general controls, application controls, and user controls.

a. Information systems general controls (entity-wide, system, and application levels) are the policies and procedures that apply to all or a large segment of an entity's information systems. General controls help ensure the proper operation of information systems by creating the environment for proper operation of application controls. General controls include security management, logical and physical access, configuration management, segregation of duties, and contingency planning.

b. Application controls, sometimes referred to as business process controls, are those controls that are incorporated directly into computer applications to help ensure the validity, completeness, accuracy, and confidentiality of transactions and data during application processing. Application controls include controls over input, processing, output, master file, interface, and the data management system.

c. User controls are portions of controls that are performed by people interacting with information systems controls. A user control is an information systems control if its effectiveness depends on information systems processing or the reliability (accuracy, completeness, and validity) of information processed by information systems.

8.64 An entity's use of information systems controls may be extensive; however, auditors are primarily interested in those information systems controls that are significant to the audit objectives. Information systems controls are significant to the audit objectives if auditors determine that it is necessary to evaluate the effectiveness of these controls in order to obtain sufficient, appropriate evidence. For example, an audit objective may involve evaluating the effectiveness of information systems controls related to certain systems, facilities, or entities.

8.65 Audit procedures to evaluate the effectiveness of significant information systems controls include (1) gaining an understanding of the system as it relates to the information and (2) identifying and evaluating the general, application, and user controls that are critical to providing assurance over the reliability of the information required for the audit.

Chapter 8: Fieldwork Standards for
Performance Audits

8.66 The evaluation of information systems controls may be done in conjunction with the auditors' consideration of internal control within the context of the audit objectives or as a separate audit objective or audit procedure, depending on the audit's objectives. Depending on the significance of information systems controls to the audit objectives, the extent of audit procedures to obtain such an understanding may be limited or extensive. In addition, the nature and extent of audit risk related to information systems controls are affected by the hardware and software used, the configuration of the entity's systems and networks, and the entity's information systems strategy.

8.67 The following factors may assist auditors in determining the significance of information system controls to the audit objectives:

a. The extent to which internal controls that are significant to the audit depend on the reliability of information processed or generated by information systems.

b. The availability of evidence outside the information system to support the findings and conclusions. It may not be possible for auditors to obtain sufficient, appropriate evidence without evaluating the effectiveness of relevant information systems controls. For example, if information supporting the findings and conclusions is generated by information systems or its reliability depends on information systems controls, there may not be sufficient supporting or corroborating information or documentary evidence available other than that produced by the information systems.

c. The relationship of information systems controls to data reliability. To obtain evidence about the reliability of computer-generated information, auditors may decide to evaluate the effectiveness of information systems controls as part of obtaining evidence about the reliability of the data. If the auditors conclude that information systems controls are effective, they may reduce the direct testing of data.

Provisions of Laws, Regulations, Contracts, and Grant Agreements

Requirement: Provisions of Laws, Regulations, Contracts, and Grant Agreements

8.68 Auditors should identify any provisions of laws, regulations, contracts, and grant agreements that are significant within the context of the audit objectives and assess the risk that noncompliance with provisions of laws, regulations, contracts, and grant agreements could occur. Based on that risk assessment, the auditors should design and perform procedures to obtain reasonable assurance of detecting instances of noncompliance with provisions of laws, regulations, contracts, and grant agreements that are significant within the context of the audit objectives.

Application Guidance: Provisions of Laws, Regulations, Contracts, and Grant Agreements

8.69 Government programs are subject to many provisions of laws, regulations, contracts, and grant agreements. At the same time, these provisions' significance within the context of the audit objectives varies widely, depending on the objectives of the audit. Auditors may consult with their legal counsel to (1) determine those laws and regulations that are significant to the audit objectives, (2) design tests of compliance with provisions of laws and regulations, and (3) evaluate the results of those tests. Auditors also may consult with their legal counsel when audit objectives require testing compliance with provisions of contracts or grant agreements. Depending on the circumstances of the audit, auditors may consult with others, such as investigative staff, other audit organizations or government entities that provided professional services to the audited entity, or law enforcement authorities, to obtain information on compliance matters.

8.70 The auditors' assessment of audit risk may be affected by such factors as the complexity or recent establishment of the laws, regulations, contracts, and grant agreements. The auditors' assessment of audit risk also may be affected by whether the audited entity has controls that are effective in preventing or detecting noncompliance with provisions of laws, regulations, contracts, and grant agreements. If auditors obtain sufficient, appropriate evidence of the effectiveness of these controls, they can reduce their tests of compliance.

Fraud

Requirements: Fraud

8.71 Auditors should assess the risk of fraud occurring that is significant within the context of the audit objectives. Audit team members should discuss among the team fraud risks, including factors such as individuals' incentives or pressures to commit fraud, the opportunity for fraud to occur, and rationalizations or attitudes that could increase the risk of fraud. Auditors should gather and assess information to identify the risk of fraud that is significant within the scope of the audit objectives or that could affect the findings and conclusions.

8.72 Assessing the risk of fraud is an ongoing process throughout the audit. When information comes to the auditors' attention indicating that fraud, significant within the context of the audit objectives, may have occurred, auditors should extend the audit steps and procedures, as necessary, to (1) determine whether fraud has likely occurred and (2) if so, determine its effect on the audit findings.

Application Guidance: Fraud

8.73 Fraud involves obtaining something of value through willful misrepresentation. Whether an act is, in fact, fraud is determined through the judicial or other adjudicative system and is beyond auditors' professional responsibility.

8.74 Auditors may obtain information through discussion with officials of the audited entity or through other means to determine the susceptibility of a program to fraud, the extent to which the audited entity has implemented leading practices to manage fraud risks, the status of internal controls the audited entity has established to prevent and detect fraud, or the risk that officials of the audited entity could override internal control. An attitude of professional skepticism in assessing the risk of fraud assists auditors in assessing which factors or risks could significantly affect the audit objectives.

8.75 In some circumstances, conditions such as the following could indicate a heightened risk of fraud:

   a. economic, programmatic, or entity operating conditions that threaten the entity's financial stability, viability, or budget;

b. the nature of the entity's operations provide opportunities to engage in fraud;

c. management's monitoring of compliance with laws, regulations, and policies is inadequate;

d. the organizational structure is unstable or unnecessarily complex;

e. management communication or support for ethical standards is lacking;

f. management is willing to accept unusually high levels of risk in making significant decisions;

g. the entity has a history of impropriety, such as previous issues with fraud, questionable practices, or past audits or investigations with findings of questionable or criminal activity;

h. operating policies and procedures have not been developed or are outdated;

i. key documentation is lacking or does not exist;

j. asset accountability or safeguarding procedures are lacking;

k. a history of improper payments;

l. evidence of false or misleading information; and

m. evidence of unusual patterns and trends in contracting, procurement, acquisition, and other activities of the entity or program.

8.76 If fraud that may have occurred is not significant within the context of the audit objectives, the auditors may perform additional audit work as a separate engagement or refer the matter to other parties with oversight responsibility or jurisdiction.

Identifying Sources of Evidence and the Amount and Type of Evidence Required

Requirements: Identifying Sources of Evidence and the Amount and Type of Evidence Required

8.77 Auditors should identify potential sources of information that could be used as evidence. Auditors should determine the amount and type of evidence needed to obtain sufficient, appropriate evidence to address the audit objectives and adequately plan audit work.

8.78 Auditors should evaluate whether any lack of sufficient, appropriate evidence is caused by internal control deficiencies or other program weaknesses, and whether the lack of sufficient, appropriate evidence could be the basis for audit findings.

Application Guidance: Identifying Sources of Evidence and the Amount and Type of Evidence Required

8.79 If auditors believe it is likely that sufficient, appropriate evidence will not be available, they may revise the audit objectives or modify the scope and methodology and determine alternative procedures to obtain additional evidence or other forms of evidence to address the current audit objectives.

Using the Work of Others

Requirements: Using the Work of Others

8.80 Auditors should determine whether other auditors have conducted, or are conducting, audits that could be relevant to the current audit objectives.

8.81 If auditors use the work of other auditors, they should perform procedures that provide a sufficient basis for using that work. Auditors should obtain evidence concerning the other auditors' qualifications and independence and should determine whether the scope, quality, and timing of the audit work performed by the other auditors can be relied on in the context of the current audit objectives.[73]

---

[73] See para. 5.80 for additional discussion on using the work of other auditors and peer review reports.

> **8.82** If the engagement team intends to use the work of a specialist, it should assess the independence of the specialist.[74]

Application Guidance: Using the Work of Others

8.83 The results of other auditors' work may be useful sources of information for planning and conducting the audit. If other auditors have identified areas that warrant further audit work or follow-up, their work may influence the auditors' selection of objectives, scope, and methodology.

8.84 Internal auditing is an important part of overall governance, accountability, and internal control. A key role of many internal audit organizations is to provide assurance that internal controls are in place to adequately mitigate risks and achieve program goals and objectives. Auditors may determine that it is appropriate to use the work of the internal auditors in assessing the effectiveness of design or operation of internal controls that are significant within the context of the audit objectives.

8.85 If other auditors have completed audit work related to the objectives of the current audit, the current auditors may be able to use the work of the other auditors to support findings or conclusions for the current audit and thereby avoid duplication of effort. Procedures that auditors may perform in making this determination include reviewing the other audit report, audit plan, or audit documentation, or performing tests of the other auditors' work. The nature and extent of evidence needed will depend on the significance of the other auditors' work to the current audit objectives and the extent to which the auditors will use that work.

8.86 The engagement team's assessment of the independence of specialists who perform audit work includes identifying threats and applying any necessary safeguards in the same manner as they would for auditors performing work on those audits.[75]

---

[74]See para. 1.27p for the definition of specialist.

[75]See paras. 3.18 through 3.108 for requirements and guidance related to independence.

Chapter 8: Fieldwork Standards for
Performance Audits

Supervision

Requirement: Supervision

8.87 Auditors must properly supervise audit staff.

Application Guidance: Supervision

8.88 Audit supervision involves providing sufficient guidance and direction to auditors assigned to the audit to address the audit objectives and follow applicable requirements, while staying informed about significant problems encountered, reviewing the work performed, and providing effective on-the-job training.

8.89 The nature and extent of the auditors' supervision and the review of audit work may vary depending on a number of factors, such as the size of the audit organization, the significance of the work, and the experience of the auditors.

Evidence

Requirements: Evidence

8.90 Auditors must obtain sufficient, appropriate evidence to provide a reasonable basis for addressing the audit objectives and supporting their findings and conclusions.

8.91 In assessing the appropriateness of evidence, auditors should assess whether the evidence is relevant, valid, and reliable.

8.92 In determining the sufficiency of evidence, auditors should determine whether enough appropriate evidence exists to address the audit objectives and support the findings and conclusions to the extent that would persuade a knowledgeable person that the findings are reasonable.

8.93 When auditors use information provided by officials of the audited entity as part of their evidence, they should determine what the officials of the audited entity or other auditors did to obtain assurance over the reliability of the information.

8.94 Auditors should evaluate the objectivity, credibility, and reliability of testimonial evidence.

Application Guidance: Evidence

8.95 Audit objectives may vary widely, as may the level of work necessary to assess the sufficiency and appropriateness of evidence to address the objectives. The concepts of audit risk and significance assist auditors in evaluating the audit evidence. Professional judgment assists auditors in determining the sufficiency and appropriateness of evidence taken as a whole. Interpreting, summarizing, or analyzing evidence is typically used in determining the sufficiency and appropriateness of evidence and in reporting the results of the audit work.

8.96 When auditors use information that audited entity officials provided as part of their evidence, auditors may find it necessary to test management's procedures to obtain assurance, perform direct testing of the information, or obtain additional corroborating evidence. The nature, timing, and extent of the auditors' procedures will depend on the significance of the information to the audit objectives and the nature of the information being used. Using a risk-based approach, auditors may consider additional procedures if they become aware of evidence that conflicts with that provided by management. In their overall assessment, auditors may document how they resolved situations involving conflicting evidence.[76]

8.97 Auditors may request that management provide written representations as to the accuracy and completeness of information provided.

8.98 The nature, timing, and extent of audit procedures to assess sufficiency and appropriateness are affected by the effectiveness of the audited entity's internal controls over the information, including information systems controls, and the significance of the information and the level of detail presented in the auditors' findings and conclusions in the context of the audit objectives. The sufficiency and appropriateness of computer-processed information is assessed regardless of whether this information is provided to auditors or auditors independently extract it. Assessing the sufficiency and appropriateness of computer-processed information includes considering the completeness and accuracy of the data for the intended purposes.

---

[76]See para. 8.105 for a discussion of the relationship between testimonial and documentary evidence.

Chapter 8: Fieldwork Standards for Performance Audits

Sufficiency

8.99 Sufficiency is a measure of the quantity of evidence used to support the findings and conclusions related to the audit objectives.

8.100 When appropriate, auditors may use statistical methods to analyze and interpret evidence to assess its sufficiency.

8.101 The sufficiency of evidence required to support the auditors' findings and conclusions is a matter of the auditors' professional judgment. The following presumptions are useful in judging the sufficiency of evidence.

    a. The greater the audit risk, the greater the quantity and quality of evidence required.

    b. Stronger evidence may allow less evidence to be used.

Appropriateness

8.102 Appropriateness is the measure of the quality of evidence that encompasses the relevance, validity, and reliability of evidence used for addressing the audit objectives and supporting findings and conclusions.

    a. Relevance refers to the extent to which evidence has a logical relationship with, and importance to, the issue being addressed.

    b. Validity refers to the extent to which evidence is a meaningful or reasonable basis for measuring what is being evaluated. In other words, validity refers to the extent to which evidence represents what it is purported to represent.

    c. Reliability refers to the consistency of results when information is measured or tested and includes the concepts of being verifiable or supported. For example, in establishing the appropriateness of evidence, auditors may test its reliability by obtaining supporting evidence, using statistical testing, or obtaining corroborating evidence.

    d. Having a large volume of evidence does not compensate for a lack of relevance, validity, or reliability.

8.103 The degree of assurance associated with a performance audit is strongly associated with the appropriateness of evidence in relation to the audit objectives. Examples follow.

   a. The audit objectives might focus on verifying specific quantitative results presented by the audited entity. In these situations, the audit procedures would likely focus on obtaining evidence about the accuracy of the specific amounts in question. This work may include the use of statistical sampling.

   b. The audit objectives might focus on the performance of a specific program or activity in the audited entity. In these situations, the auditors may be provided information that the audited entity compiled in order to satisfy the audit objectives. The auditors may find it necessary to test the quality of the information, which includes both its validity and reliability.

   c. The audit objectives might focus on information that is used for widely accepted purposes and obtained from sources generally recognized as appropriate. For example, economic statistics issued by government agencies for purposes such as adjusting for inflation, or other such information issued by authoritative organizations, may be the best information available. In such cases, it may not be practical or necessary for auditors to perform procedures to verify the information. These decisions call for use of professional judgment based on the nature of the information, its common usage or acceptance, and how it is being used in the audit.

   d. The audit objectives might focus on comparisons or benchmarking between various government functions or agencies. These types of audits are especially useful for analyzing the outcomes of various public policy decisions. In these cases, auditors may perform analyses, such as comparative statistics of different jurisdictions or changes in performance over time, where it would be impractical to verify the detailed data underlying the statistics. Clear disclosure of the extent to which comparative information or statistics were evaluated or corroborated will likely be necessary to place the evidence in context for report users.

   e. The audit objectives might focus on trend information based on data that the audited entity provided. In this situation, auditors may assess the evidence by using overall analytical tests of underlying

**Chapter 8: Fieldwork Standards for
Performance Audits**

data, combined with knowledge and understanding of the systems or processes used for compiling information.

f. The audit objectives might focus on identifying emerging and crosscutting issues using information that audited entities compiled or self-reported. In such cases, it may be helpful for the auditors to consider the overall appropriateness of the compiled information along with other information available about the program. Other sources of information, such as inspector general reports or other external audits, may provide the auditors with information regarding whether any unverified or self-reported information is consistent with or can be corroborated by these other external sources of information.

8.104 In terms of its form and how it is collected, evidence may be categorized as physical, documentary, or testimonial. Physical evidence is obtained by auditors' direct inspection or observation of people, property, or events. Such evidence may be documented in summary memos, photographs, videos, drawings, charts, maps, or physical samples. Documentary evidence is already existing information, such as letters, contracts, accounting records, invoices, spreadsheets, database extracts, electronically stored information, and management information on performance. Testimonial evidence is obtained through inquiries, interviews, focus groups, public forums, or questionnaires. Auditors frequently use analytical processes, including computations, comparisons, separation of information into components, and rational arguments, to analyze any evidence gathered to determine whether it is sufficient and appropriate. Evidence may be obtained by observation, inquiry, or inspection. Each type of evidence has its own strengths and weaknesses. The following contrasts are useful in judging the appropriateness of evidence. However, these contrasts are not adequate in themselves to determine appropriateness. The nature and types of evidence used to support auditors' findings and conclusions are matters of the auditors' professional judgment based on the audit objectives and audit risk.

a. Evidence obtained when internal control is effective is generally more reliable than evidence obtained when internal control is weak or nonexistent.[77]

---

[77]See paras. 8.39 through 8.67 for a discussion of internal control.

b. Evidence obtained through the auditors' direct physical examination, observation, computation, and inspection is generally more reliable than evidence obtained indirectly.

c. Examination of original documents is generally more reliable than examination of copies.

d. Testimonial evidence obtained under conditions in which persons may speak freely is generally more reliable than evidence obtained under circumstances in which the persons may be intimidated.

e. Testimonial evidence obtained from an individual who is not biased and has direct knowledge about the area is generally more reliable than testimonial evidence obtained from an individual who is biased or has indirect or partial knowledge about the area.

f. Evidence obtained from a knowledgeable, credible, and unbiased third party is generally more reliable than evidence obtained from management of the audited entity or others who have a direct interest in the audited entity.

8.105 Testimonial evidence may be useful in interpreting or corroborating documentary or physical information. Documentary evidence may be used to help verify, support, or challenge testimonial evidence.

8.106 Surveys generally provide self-reported information about existing conditions or programs. Evaluating the survey design and administration assists auditors in evaluating the objectivity, credibility, and reliability of the self-reported information.

8.107 When sampling is used, the appropriate selection method will depend on the audit objectives. When a representative sample is needed, the use of statistical sampling approaches generally results in stronger evidence than that obtained from nonstatistical techniques. When a representative sample is not needed, a targeted selection may be effective if the auditors have isolated risk factors or other criteria to target the selection.

Overall Assessment of Evidence

Requirements: Overall Assessment of Evidence

8.108 Auditors should perform and document an overall assessment of the collective evidence used to support findings and conclusions, including the results of any specific assessments performed to conclude on the validity and reliability of specific evidence.

8.109 When assessing the overall sufficiency and appropriateness of evidence, auditors should evaluate the expected significance of evidence to the audit objectives, findings, and conclusions; available corroborating evidence; and the level of audit risk. If auditors conclude that evidence is not sufficient or appropriate, they should not use such evidence as support for findings and conclusions.

8.110 When the auditors identify limitations or uncertainties in evidence that is significant to the audit findings and conclusions, they should perform additional procedures, as appropriate.

Application Guidance: Overall Assessment of Evidence

8.111 Professional judgments about the sufficiency and appropriateness of evidence are closely interrelated, as auditors interpret the results of audit testing and evaluate whether the nature and extent of the evidence obtained is sufficient and appropriate.

8.112 Sufficiency and appropriateness of evidence are relative concepts, which may be thought of as a continuum rather than as absolutes. Sufficiency and appropriateness are evaluated in the context of the related findings and conclusions. For example, even though the auditors may identify some limitations or uncertainties about the sufficiency or appropriateness of some of the evidence, they may nonetheless determine that in total there is sufficient, appropriate evidence to support the findings and conclusions.

8.113 The steps to assess evidence may depend on the nature of the evidence, how the evidence is used in the audit or report, and the audit objectives.

   a. Evidence is sufficient and appropriate when it provides a reasonable basis for supporting the findings or conclusions within the context of the audit objectives.

b. Evidence is not sufficient or appropriate when (1) using the evidence carries an unacceptably high risk that it could lead auditors to reach an incorrect or improper conclusion; (2) the evidence has significant limitations, given the audit objectives and intended use of the evidence; or (3) the evidence does not provide an adequate basis for addressing the audit objectives or supporting the findings and conclusions.

8.114 Evidence has limitations or uncertainties when its validity or reliability has not been assessed or cannot be assessed, given the audit objectives and the intended use of the evidence. Limitations also include errors identified by the auditors in their testing.

8.115 Additional procedures that could address limitations or uncertainties in evidence that are significant to the audit findings and conclusions include

a. seeking independent, corroborating evidence from other sources;

b. redefining the audit objectives or the audit scope to eliminate the need to use the evidence;

c. presenting the findings and conclusions so that the supporting evidence is sufficient and appropriate and describing in the report the limitations or uncertainties with the validity or reliability of the evidence, if such disclosure is necessary to avoid misleading the report users about the findings or conclusions; and

d. determining whether to report the limitations or uncertainties as a finding, including any related significant internal control deficiencies.

Findings

Requirements: Findings

8.116 As part of a performance audit, when auditors identify findings, they should plan and perform procedures to develop the criteria, condition, cause, and effect of the findings to the extent that these elements are relevant and necessary to achieve the audit objectives.

8.117 Auditors should consider internal control deficiencies in their

> evaluation of identified findings when developing the cause element of the identified findings when internal control is significant to the audit objectives.

Application Guidance: Findings

8.118 Findings may involve deficiencies in internal control; noncompliance with provisions of laws, regulations, contracts, and grant agreements; or instances of fraud.

8.119 Given the concept of accountability for use of public resources and government authority, evaluating internal control in a government environment may also include considering internal control deficiencies that result in waste or abuse. Because the determination of waste and abuse is subjective, auditors are not required to perform specific procedures to detect waste or abuse in performance audits. However, auditors may consider whether and how to communicate such matters if they become aware of them. Auditors may also discover that waste or abuse are indicative of fraud or noncompliance with provisions of laws, regulations, contracts, and grant agreements.

8.120 Waste is the act of using or expending resources carelessly, extravagantly, or to no purpose. Importantly, waste can include activities that do not include abuse and does not necessarily involve a violation of law. Rather, waste relates primarily to mismanagement, inappropriate actions, and inadequate oversight.

8.121 The following are examples of waste, depending on the facts and circumstances:

   a. Making travel choices that are contrary to existing travel policies or are unnecessarily extravagant or expensive.

   b. Making procurement or vendor selections that are contrary to existing policies or are unnecessarily extravagant or expensive.

8.122 Abuse is behavior that is deficient or improper when compared with behavior that a prudent person would consider reasonable and necessary business practice given the facts and circumstances, but excludes fraud and noncompliance with provisions of laws, regulations, contracts, and grant agreements. Abuse also includes misuse of authority or position for personal financial interests or those of an immediate or close family member or business associate.

8.123 The following are examples of abuse, depending on the facts and circumstances:

a. Creating unneeded overtime.

b. Requesting staff to perform personal errands or work tasks for a supervisor or manager.

c. Misusing the official's position for personal gain (including actions that could be perceived by an objective third party with knowledge of the relevant information as improperly benefiting an official's personal financial interests or those of an immediate or close family member; a general partner; an organization for which the official serves as an officer, director, trustee, or employee; or an organization with which the official is negotiating concerning future employment).

8.124 Criteria: To develop findings, criteria may include the laws, regulations, contracts, grant agreements, standards, measures, expected performance, defined business practices, and benchmarks against which performance is compared or evaluated. Criteria identify the required or desired state or expectation with respect to the program or operation. The term program includes processes, projects, studies, policies, operations, activities, entities, and functions. Criteria provide a context for evaluating evidence and understanding the findings, conclusions, and recommendations in the report.

8.125 Condition: Condition is a situation that exists. The condition is determined and documented during the audit.

8.126 Cause: The cause is the factor or factors responsible for the difference between the condition and the criteria, and may also serve as a basis for recommendations for corrective actions. Common factors include poorly designed policies, procedures, or criteria; inconsistent, incomplete, or incorrect implementation; or factors beyond the control of program management. Auditors may assess whether the evidence provides a reasonable and convincing argument for why the stated cause is the key factor contributing to the difference between the condition and the criteria.

Chapter 8: Fieldwork Standards for Performance Audits

8.127 Effect or potential effect: The effect or potential effect is the outcome or consequence resulting from the difference between the condition and the criteria. When the audit objectives include identifying the actual or potential consequences of a condition that varies (either positively or negatively) from the criteria identified in the audit, effect is a measure of those consequences. Effect or potential effect may be used to demonstrate the need for corrective action in response to identified problems or relevant risks.

8.128 The elements needed for a finding are related to the objectives of the audit. Thus, a finding or set of findings is complete to the extent that the audit objectives are addressed and the report clearly relates those objectives to the elements of a finding. For example, an audit objective may be to determine the current status or condition of program operations or progress in implementing legislative requirements, and not the related cause or effect. In this situation, developing the condition would address the audit objective, and developing the other elements of a finding would not be necessary.

8.129 The cause of a finding may relate to an underlying internal control deficiency. For example, auditors conducting a compliance audit may find that an audited entity has not complied with certain legislation. Upon further evaluation, the auditors may find the root cause of the finding to be that one of the entity's control activities was not properly designed. In this case, the finding would be an instance of noncompliance, but the cause of the finding would be an internal control deficiency.

8.130 Considering internal control in the context of a comprehensive internal control framework, such as *Standards for Internal Control in the Federal Government* or *Internal Control—Integrated Framework*,[78] can help auditors to determine whether underlying internal control deficiencies exist as the root cause of findings. When the audit objectives include explaining why a particular type of positive or negative program performance, output, or outcome identified in the audit occurred, the underlying deficiencies are referred to as cause. Identifying the cause of

---

[78]The COSO Framework and the Green Book provide suitable and available criteria against which management may evaluate and report on the effectiveness of the entity's internal control. The Green Book may be adopted by entities beyond those federal entities for which it is legally required, such as state, local, and quasi-governmental entities, as well as other federal entities and not-for-profit organizations, as a framework for an internal control system.

problems may assist auditors in making constructive recommendations for correction. Auditors may identify deficiencies in program design or structure as the cause of deficient performance. Auditors may also identify deficiencies in internal control that are significant to the subject matter of the performance audit as the cause of deficient performance. In developing these types of findings, the deficiencies in program design or internal control would be described as the cause. Often the causes of deficient program performance are complex and involve multiple factors, including fundamental, systemic root causes.

8.131 When the audit objectives include estimating the extent to which a program has caused changes in physical, social, or economic conditions, "effect" is a measure of the program's impact. In this case, effect is the extent to which positive or negative changes in actual physical, social, or economic conditions can be identified and attributed to the program.

Audit Documentation

Requirements: Audit Documentation

8.132 Auditors must prepare audit documentation related to planning, conducting, and reporting for each audit. Auditors should prepare audit documentation in sufficient detail to enable an experienced auditor, having no previous connection to the audit, to understand from the audit documentation the nature, timing, extent, and results of audit procedures performed; the evidence obtained; and its source and the conclusions reached, including evidence that supports the auditors' significant judgments and conclusions.

8.133 Auditors should prepare audit documentation that contains evidence that supports the findings, conclusions, and recommendations before they issue their report.

8.134 Auditors should design the form and content of audit documentation to meet the circumstances of the particular audit. The audit documentation constitutes the principal record of the work that the auditors have performed in accordance with standards and the conclusions that the auditors have reached. The quantity, type, and content of audit documentation are a matter of the auditors' professional judgment.

Chapter 8: Fieldwork Standards for
Performance Audits

> **8.135** Auditors should document the following:
>
> a. the objectives, scope, and methodology of the audit;
>
> b. the work performed and evidence obtained to support significant judgments and conclusions, as well as expectations in analytical procedures, including descriptions of transactions and records examined (for example, by listing file numbers, case numbers, or other means of identifying specific documents examined, though copies of documents examined or detailed listings of information from those documents are not required); and
>
> c. supervisory review, before the audit report is issued, of the evidence that supports the findings, conclusions, and recommendations contained in the audit report.
>
> **8.136** When auditors do not comply with applicable GAGAS requirements because of law, regulation, scope limitations, restrictions on access to records, or other issues affecting the audit, the auditors should document the departure from the GAGAS requirements and the impact on the audit and on the auditors' conclusions.

Application Guidance: Audit Documentation

8.137 Audit documentation is an essential element of audit quality. The process of preparing and reviewing audit documentation contributes to the quality of an audit. Audit documentation serves to (1) provide the principal support for the audit report, (2) aid auditors in conducting and supervising the audit, and (3) allow for the review of audit quality.

8.138 An experienced auditor means an individual (whether internal or external to the audit organization) who possesses the competencies and skills that would have enabled him or her to conduct the performance audit. These competencies and skills include an understanding of (1) the performance audit processes, (2) GAGAS and applicable legal and regulatory requirements, (3) the subject matter associated with achieving the audit objectives, and (4) issues related to the audited entity's environment.

8.139 When documenting departures from the GAGAS requirements, the audit documentation requirements apply to departures from unconditional requirements and from presumptively mandatory requirements when alternative procedures performed in the circumstances were not sufficient to achieve the objectives of the requirements.

Availability of Individuals and Documentation

Requirement: Availability of Individuals and Documentation

8.140 Subject to applicable provisions of laws and regulations, auditors should make appropriate individuals and audit documentation available upon request and in a timely manner to other auditors or reviewers.

Application Guidance: Availability of Individuals and Documentation

8.141 Underlying GAGAS audits is the premise that audit organizations in federal, state, and local governments and public accounting firms engaged to conduct audits in accordance with GAGAS cooperate in auditing programs of common interest so that auditors may use others' work and avoid duplication of efforts. The use of auditors' work by other auditors may be facilitated by contractual arrangements for GAGAS audits that provide for full and timely access to appropriate individuals and to audit documentation.

Figure 4: Consideration of Internal Control in a Generally Accepted Government Auditing Standards Performance Audit

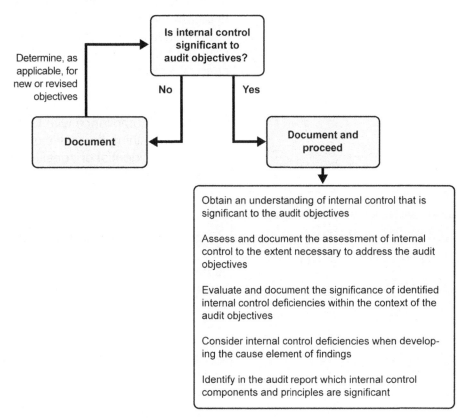

Source: GAO. | GAO-18-568G

Chapter 9: Reporting Standards for Performance Audits

9.01 This chapter contains reporting requirements and guidance for performance audits conducted in accordance with generally accepted government auditing standards (GAGAS). Reporting requirements establish the auditors' overall approach for communicating the results of a performance audit. For performance audits conducted in accordance with GAGAS, the requirements and guidance in chapters 1 through 5 and chapter 8 also apply.

9.02 The reporting requirements for performance audits relate to reporting the auditors' compliance with GAGAS, the form of the report, the report contents, obtaining the views of responsible officials, report distribution, reporting confidential or sensitive information, and discovery of insufficient evidence after report release.

Reporting Auditors' Compliance with GAGAS

Requirements: Reporting Auditors' Compliance with GAGAS

9.03 When auditors comply with all applicable GAGAS requirements, they should use the following language, which represents an unmodified GAGAS compliance statement, in the audit report to indicate that they conducted the audit in accordance with GAGAS:

We conducted this performance audit in accordance with generally accepted government auditing standards. Those standards require that we plan and perform the audit to obtain sufficient, appropriate evidence to provide a reasonable basis for our findings and conclusions based on our audit objectives. We believe that the evidence obtained provides a reasonable basis for our findings and conclusions based on our audit objectives.

9.04 Audit organizations that meet the independence requirements for internal audit organizations, but not those for external audit organizations, should include in the GAGAS compliance statement, where applicable, a statement that they are independent per the GAGAS requirements for internal auditors.

9.05 When auditors do not comply with all applicable GAGAS requirements, they should include a modified GAGAS compliance statement in the audit report. For performance audits, auditors should use a statement that includes either (1) the language in paragraph

9.03, modified to indicate the requirements that were not followed, or (2) language indicating that the auditors did not follow GAGAS.

Report Format

Requirements: Report Format

9.06 Auditors should issue audit reports communicating the results of each completed performance audit.

9.07 Auditors should issue the audit report in a form that is appropriate for its intended use, either in writing or in some other retrievable form.[79]

Application Guidance: Report Format

9.08 The purposes of audit reports are to (1) clearly communicate the results of audits to those charged with governance, the appropriate officials of the audited entity, and the appropriate oversight officials and (2) facilitate follow-up to determine whether appropriate corrective actions have been taken.

9.09 Auditors may present audit reports using electronic media through which report users and the audit organization can retrieve them. The users' needs will influence the form of the audit report. Different forms of audit reports include written reports, letters, briefing slides, or other presentation materials.

Report Content

Requirements: Report Content, Including Objectives, Scope, and Methodology

9.10 Auditors should prepare audit reports that contain (1) the objectives, scope, and methodology of the audit; (2) the audit results, including findings, conclusions, and recommendations, as appropriate;

---

[79]See paras. 9.56 through 9.67 for a discussion of report distribution and reporting confidential or sensitive information.

(3) a summary of the views of responsible officials; and (4) if applicable, the nature of any confidential or sensitive information omitted.

9.11 Auditors should communicate audit objectives in the audit report in a clear, specific, neutral, and unbiased manner that includes relevant assumptions. In order to avoid potential misunderstanding, when audit objectives are limited but users could infer broader objectives, auditors should state in the audit report that certain issues were outside the scope of the audit.

9.12 Auditors should describe the scope of the work performed and any limitations, including issues that would be relevant to likely users, so that report users can reasonably interpret the findings, conclusions, and recommendations in the report without being misled. Auditors should also report any significant constraints imposed on the audit approach by information limitations or scope impairments, including denials of, or excessive delays in, access to certain records or individuals.

9.13 In describing the work performed to address the audit objectives and support the reported findings and conclusions, auditors should, as applicable, explain the relationship between the population and the items tested; identify entities, geographic locations, and the period covered; report the kinds and sources of evidence; and explain any significant limitations or uncertainties based on the auditors' overall assessment of the sufficiency and appropriateness of the evidence in the aggregate.

9.14 In reporting audit methodology, auditors should explain how the completed audit work supports the audit objectives, including the evidence-gathering and evidence-analysis techniques, in sufficient detail to allow knowledgeable users of their reports to understand how the auditors addressed the audit objectives. Auditors should identify significant assumptions made in conducting the audit; describe comparative techniques applied; describe the criteria used; and, when the results of sample testing significantly support the auditors' findings, conclusions, or recommendations, describe the sample design and state why the design was chosen, including whether the results can be projected to the intended population.

Application Guidance: Report Content, Including Objectives, Scope, and Methodology

9.15 Report users need information regarding the audit objectives, scope, and methodology to understand the purpose of the audit; the nature and extent of the audit work performed; the context and perspective regarding what is reported; and any significant limitations in the audit objectives, scope, or methodology.

9.16 In reporting audit methodology, auditors may include a description of the procedures performed as part of their assessment of the sufficiency and appropriateness of information used as audit evidence.

9.17 The auditor may use the report quality elements of accurate, objective, complete, convincing, clear, concise, and timely when developing and writing the audit report as the subject permits.

   a. Accurate: An accurate report is supported by sufficient, appropriate evidence with key facts, figures, and findings being traceable to the audit evidence. Reports that are fact-based, with a clear statement of sources, methods, and assumptions so that report users can judge how much weight to give the evidence reported, assist in achieving accuracy. Disclosing data limitations and other disclosures also contribute to producing more accurate audit reports. Reports also are more accurate when the findings are presented in the broader context of the issue. One way to help the audit organization prepare accurate audit reports is to use a quality control process such as referencing. Referencing is a process in which an experienced auditor who is independent of the audit checks that statements of facts, figures, and dates are correctly reported; the findings are adequately supported by the evidence in the audit documentation; and the conclusions and recommendations flow logically from the evidence.

   b. Objective: Objective means that the presentation of the report is balanced in content and tone. A report's credibility is significantly enhanced when it presents evidence in an unbiased manner and in the proper context. This means presenting the audit results impartially and fairly. The tone of reports may encourage decision makers to act on the auditors' findings and recommendations. This balanced tone can be achieved when reports present sufficient, appropriate evidence to support conclusions while refraining from using adjectives or adverbs that characterize evidence in a way that implies criticism or unsupported conclusions. The objectivity of audit reports is enhanced when the report explicitly states the source of the evidence and the assumptions used in the analysis. The report may recognize the positive aspects of the program reviewed if applicable to the audit objectives. Inclusion of positive program aspects may lead to improved performance by other government organizations that read the report. Audit reports are more objective when they demonstrate that the work has been performed by professional, unbiased, independent, and knowledgeable personnel.

c. Complete: Being complete means that the report contains sufficient, appropriate evidence needed to satisfy the audit objectives and promote an understanding of the matters reported. It also means the report states evidence and findings without omission of significant relevant information related to the audit objectives. Providing report users with an understanding means providing perspective on the extent and significance of reported findings, such as the frequency of occurrence relative to the number of cases or transactions tested and the relationship of the findings to the entity's operations. Being complete also means clearly stating what was and was not done and explicitly describing data limitations, constraints imposed by restrictions on access to records, or other issues.

d. Convincing: Being convincing means that the audit results are responsive to the audit objectives, that the findings are presented persuasively, and that the conclusions and recommendations flow logically from the facts presented. The validity of the findings, the reasonableness of the conclusions, and the benefit of implementing the recommendations are more convincing when supported by sufficient, appropriate evidence. Reports designed in this way can help focus the attention of responsible officials on the matters that warrant attention and can provide an incentive for taking corrective action.

e. Clear: Clarity means the report is easy for the intended user to read and understand. Preparing the report in language as clear and simple as the subject permits assists auditors in achieving this goal. Use of straightforward, nontechnical language is helpful to simplify presentation. Defining technical terms, abbreviations, and acronyms that are used in the report is also helpful. Auditors may use a highlights page or summary within the report to capture the

Chapter 9: Reporting Standards for
Performance Audits

report user's attention and highlight the overall message. If a summary is used, it is helpful if it focuses on the audit objectives, summarizes the audit's most significant findings and the report's principal conclusions, and prepares users to anticipate the major recommendations. Logical organization of material and accuracy and precision in stating facts and in drawing conclusions assist in the report's clarity and understandability. Effective use of titles and captions and topic sentences makes the report easier to read and understand. Visual aids (such as pictures, charts, graphs, and maps) may help clarify and summarize complex material.

f. Concise: Being concise means that the report is no longer than necessary to convey and support the message. Extraneous detail detracts from a report and may even conceal the real message and confuse or distract the users. Although room exists for considerable judgment in determining the content of reports, those that are fact-based but concise are likely to achieve results.

g. Timely: To be of maximum use, providing relevant evidence in time to respond to officials of the audited entity, legislative officials, and other users' legitimate needs is the auditors' goal. Likewise, the evidence provided in the report is more helpful if it is current. Therefore, the timely issuance of the report is an important reporting goal for auditors. During the audit, the auditors may provide interim reports of significant matters to appropriate entity and oversight officials. Such communication alerts officials to matters needing immediate attention and allows them to take corrective action before the final report is completed.

Reporting Findings, Conclusions, and Recommendations

Requirements: Reporting Findings, Conclusions, and Recommendations

9.18 In the audit report, auditors should present sufficient, appropriate evidence to support the findings and conclusions in relation to the audit objectives. Auditors should provide recommendations for corrective action if findings are significant within the context of the audit objectives.

9.19 Auditors should report conclusions based on the audit objectives and the audit findings.

Chapter 9: Reporting Standards for
Performance Audits

9.20 Auditors should describe in their report limitations or uncertainties with the reliability or validity of evidence if (1) the evidence is significant to the findings and conclusions within the context of the audit objectives and (2) such disclosure is necessary to avoid misleading the report users about the findings and conclusions. Auditors should describe the limitations or uncertainties regarding evidence in conjunction with the findings and conclusions, in addition to describing those limitations or uncertainties as part of the objectives, scope, and methodology.

9.21 Auditors should place their findings in perspective by describing the nature and extent of the issues being reported and the extent of the work performed that resulted in the findings. To give the reader a basis for judging the prevalence and consequences of these findings, auditors should, as appropriate, relate the instances identified to the population or the number of cases examined and quantify the results in terms of dollar value or other measures. If the results cannot be projected, auditors should limit their conclusions appropriately.

9.22 When reporting on the results of their work, auditors should disclose significant facts relevant to the objectives of their work and known to them that if not disclosed could mislead knowledgeable users, misrepresent the results, or conceal significant improper or illegal practices.

9.23 When feasible, auditors should recommend actions to correct deficiencies and other findings identified during the audit and to improve programs and operations when the potential for improvement in programs, operations, and performance is substantiated by the reported findings and conclusions. Auditors should make recommendations that flow logically from the findings and conclusions, are directed at resolving the cause of identified deficiencies and findings, and clearly state the actions recommended.

Application Guidance: Reporting Findings, Conclusions, and Recommendations

9.24 The extent to which the elements for a finding are developed depends on the audit objectives. Clearly developed findings assist management and oversight officials of the audited entity in understanding the need for taking corrective action.

9.25 As discussed in paragraphs 8.108 through 8.115, even though the auditors may have some uncertainty about the sufficiency or appropriateness of some of the evidence, they may nonetheless determine that in total there is sufficient, appropriate evidence given the findings and conclusions. Describing limitations provides report users with a clear understanding of how much responsibility the auditors are taking for the information.

9.26 Auditors may provide background information to establish the context for the overall message and to help the reader understand the findings and significance of the issues discussed. Appropriate background information may include information on how programs and operations work; the significance of programs and operations (e.g., dollars, effect, purposes, and past audit work, if relevant); a description of the audited entity's responsibilities; and explanation of terms, organizational structure, and the statutory basis for the program and operations.

9.27 Report conclusions are logical inferences about the program based on the auditors' findings, not merely a summary of the findings. The strength of the auditors' conclusions depends on the persuasiveness of the evidence supporting the findings and the soundness of the logic used to formulate the conclusions. Conclusions are more compelling if they lead to recommendations and convince a knowledgeable user of the report that action is necessary.

9.28 Effective recommendations encourage improvements in the conduct of government programs and operations. Recommendations are effective when they are addressed to parties with the authority to act and when the recommended actions are specific, feasible, cost-effective, and measurable.

Reporting on Internal Control

Requirements: Reporting on Internal Control

9.29 When internal control is significant within the context of the audit objectives, auditors should include in the audit report (1) the scope of their work on internal control and (2) any deficiencies in internal control that are significant within the context of the audit objectives and based upon the audit work performed.

Chapter 9: Reporting Standards for Performance Audits

> **9.30** If some but not all internal control components are significant to the audit objectives, the auditors should identify as part of the scope those internal control components and underlying principles that are significant to the audit objectives.
>
> **9.31** When auditors detect deficiencies in internal control that are not significant to the objectives of the audit but warrant the attention of those charged with governance, they should include those deficiencies either in the report or communicate those deficiencies in writing to audited entity officials. If the written communication is separate from the audit report, auditors should refer to that written communication in the audit report.

Application Guidance: Reporting on Internal Control

9.32 Control components and underlying principles that are not considered significant to the audit objectives may be identified in the scope if, in the auditors' professional judgment, doing so is necessary to preclude a misunderstanding of the breadth of the conclusions of the audit report and to clarify that control effectiveness has not been evaluated as a whole. Auditors may also identify and describe the five components of internal control so that report users understand the scope of the work within the context of the entity's internal control system.

9.33 An internal control system is effective if the five components of internal control are effectively designed, implemented, and operating, and are operating together in an integrated manner. The principles support the effective design, implementation, and operation of the associated components and represent requirements necessary to establish an effective internal control system. If a principle is not applied effectively, then the respective component cannot be effective. If a principle or component is not effective, or the components are not operating together in an integrated manner, then an internal control system cannot be effective.

9.34 When auditors detect deficiencies in internal control that do not warrant the attention of those charged with governance, determining whether and how to communicate such deficiencies to audited entity officials is a matter of professional judgment.

Reporting on Noncompliance with Provisions of Laws, Regulations, Contracts, and Grant Agreements

Requirements: Reporting on Noncompliance with Provisions of Laws, Regulations, Contracts, and Grant Agreements

9.35 Auditors should report a matter as a finding when they conclude, based on sufficient, appropriate evidence, that noncompliance with provisions of laws, regulations, contracts, and grant agreements either has occurred or is likely to have occurred that is significant within the context of the audit objectives.

9.36 Auditors should communicate findings in writing to audited entity officials when the auditors detect instances of noncompliance with provisions of laws, regulations, contracts, and grant agreements that are not significant within the context of the audit objectives but warrant the attention of those charged with governance.

Application Guidance: Reporting on Noncompliance with Provisions of Laws, Regulations, Contracts, and Grant Agreements

9.37 Whether a particular act is, in fact, noncompliance with provisions of laws, regulations, contracts, and grant agreements may have to await final determination by a court of law or other adjudicative body.[80]

9.38 When auditors detect instances of noncompliance with provisions of laws, regulations, contracts, and grant agreements that do not warrant the attention of those charged with governance, the auditors' determination of whether and how to communicate such instances to audited entity officials is a matter of professional judgment.

9.39 When noncompliance with provisions of laws, regulations, contracts, and grant agreements either has occurred or is likely to have occurred, auditors may consult with authorities or legal counsel about whether publicly reporting such information would compromise investigative or legal proceedings. Auditors may limit their public reporting to matters that would not compromise those proceedings and, for example, report only on information that is already a part of the public record.

---

[80]See paras. 8.27 through 8.29 for a discussion of investigations or legal proceedings.

Chapter 9: Reporting Standards for
Performance Audits

Reporting on Instances of Fraud

Requirements: Reporting on Instances of Fraud

9.40 Auditors should report a matter as a finding when they conclude, based on sufficient, appropriate evidence, that fraud either has occurred or is likely to have occurred that is significant to the audit objectives.

9.41 Auditors should communicate findings in writing to audited entity officials when the auditors detect instances of fraud that are not significant within the context of the audit objectives but warrant the attention of those charged with governance.

Application Guidance: Reporting on Instances of Fraud

9.42 Whether a particular act is, in fact, fraud may have to await final determination by a court of law or other adjudicative body.[81]

9.43 When auditors detect instances of fraud that do not warrant the attention of those charged with governance, the auditors' determination of whether and how to communicate such instances to audited entity officials is a matter of professional judgment.

9.44 When auditors conclude fraud has occurred or is likely to have occurred, auditors may consult with authorities or legal counsel about whether publicly reporting such information would compromise investigative or legal proceedings. Auditors may limit their public reporting to matters that would not compromise those proceedings and, for example, report only on information that is already a part of the public record.

Reporting Findings Directly to Parties outside the Audited Entity

Requirements: Reporting Findings Directly to Parties outside the Audited Entity

9.45 Auditors should report known or likely noncompliance with provisions of laws, regulations, contracts, and grant agreements or fraud directly to parties outside the audited entity in the following two

---

[81] See paras. 8.27 through 8.29 for a discussion of investigations or legal proceedings.

circumstances.

a. When audited entity management fails to satisfy legal or regulatory requirements to report such information to external parties specified in law or regulation, auditors should first communicate the failure to report such information to those charged with governance. If the audited entity still does not report this information to the specified external parties as soon as practicable after the auditors' communication with those charged with governance, then the auditors should report the information directly to the specified external parties.

b. When audited entity management fails to take timely and appropriate steps to respond to noncompliance with provisions of laws, regulations, contracts, and grant agreements or instances of fraud that (1) are likely to have a significant effect on the subject matter and (2) involve funding received directly or indirectly from a government agency, auditors should first report management's failure to take timely and appropriate steps to those charged with governance. If the audited entity still does not take timely and appropriate steps as soon as practicable after the auditors' communication with those charged with governance, then the auditors should report the audited entity's failure to take timely and appropriate steps directly to the funding agency.

9.46 Auditors should comply with the requirements in paragraph 9.45 even if they have resigned or been dismissed from the audit prior to its completion.

9.47 Auditors should obtain sufficient, appropriate evidence, such as confirmation from outside parties, to corroborate representations by audited entity management that it has reported audit findings in accordance with provisions of laws, regulations, or funding agreements. When auditors are unable to do so, they should report such information directly, as discussed in paragraphs 9.45 and 9.46.

Application Guidance: Reporting Findings Directly to Parties outside the Audited Entity

9.48 The reporting in paragraph 9.45 is in addition to any legal requirements to report such information directly to parties outside the audited entity.

9.49 Internal audit organizations do not have a duty to report outside the audited entity unless required by law, regulation, or policy.

Obtaining the Views of Responsible Officials

Requirements: Obtaining the Views of Responsible Officials

9.50 Auditors should obtain and report the views of responsible officials of the audited entity concerning the findings, conclusions, and recommendations in the audit report, as well as any planned corrective actions.

9.51 When auditors receive written comments from the responsible officials, they should include in their report a copy of the officials' written comments or a summary of the comments received. When the responsible officials provide oral comments only, auditors should prepare a summary of the oral comments, provide a copy of the summary to the responsible officials to verify that the comments are accurately represented, and include the summary in their report.

9.52 When the audited entity's comments are inconsistent or in conflict with the findings, conclusions, or recommendations in the draft report, the auditors should evaluate the validity of the audited entity's comments. If the auditors disagree with the comments, they should explain in the report their reasons for disagreement. Conversely, the auditors should modify their report as necessary if they find the comments valid and supported by sufficient, appropriate evidence.

9.53 If the audited entity refuses to provide comments or is unable to provide comments within a reasonable period of time, the auditors may issue the report without receiving comments from the audited entity. In such cases, the auditors should indicate in the report that the audited entity did not provide comments.

Application Guidance: Obtaining the Views of Responsible Officials

9.54 Providing a draft report with findings for review and comment by responsible officials of the audited entity and others helps the auditors develop a report that is fair, complete, and objective. Including the views of responsible officials results in a report that presents not only the auditors' findings, conclusions, and recommendations, but also the perspectives of the audited entity's responsible officials and the corrective actions they plan to take. Obtaining the comments in writing is preferred, but oral comments are acceptable. In cases in which the audited entity provides technical comments in addition to its written or oral comments on the report, auditors may disclose in the report that such comments were received. Technical comments address points of fact or are editorial in nature and do not address substantive issues, such as methodology, findings, conclusions, or recommendations.

9.55 Obtaining oral comments may be appropriate when, for example, there is a reporting date critical to meeting a user's needs; auditors have worked closely with the responsible officials throughout the engagement, and the parties are familiar with the findings and issues addressed in the draft report; or the auditors do not expect major disagreements with findings, conclusions, or recommendations in the draft report, or major controversies with regard to the issues discussed in the draft report.

Report Distribution

Requirements: Report Distribution

9.56 Distribution of reports completed in accordance with GAGAS depends on the auditors' relationship with the audited organization and the nature of the information contained in the reports. Auditors should document any limitation on report distribution. Auditors should make audit reports available to the public, unless distribution is specifically limited by the terms of the engagement, law, or regulation.

Report Distribution for Internal Auditors

9.57 If an internal audit organization in a government entity follows the Institute of Internal Auditors' *International Standards for the Professional Practice of Internal Auditing* as well as GAGAS, the head of the internal audit organization should communicate results to the parties who can ensure that the results are given due consideration. If not otherwise mandated by statutory or regulatory requirements, prior to releasing results to parties outside the organization, the head of the internal audit organization should (1) assess the potential risk to the organization, (2) consult with senior management or legal counsel as appropriate, and (3) control dissemination by indicating the intended users in the report.

Report Distribution for External Auditors

9.58 An audit organization in a government entity should distribute audit reports to those charged with governance, to the appropriate audited entity officials, and to the appropriate oversight bodies or organizations requiring or arranging for the audits. As appropriate, auditors should also distribute copies of the reports to other officials who have legal oversight authority or who may be responsible for acting on audit findings and recommendations and to others authorized to receive such reports.

9.59 A public accounting firm contracted to conduct an audit in accordance with GAGAS should clarify report distribution responsibilities with the engaging party. If the contracting firm is responsible for the distribution, it should reach agreement with the party contracting for the audit about which officials or organizations will receive the report and the steps being taken to make the report available to the public.

Application Guidance: Report Distribution for External Auditors

9.60 Making an audit report available to the public can involve auditors posting the audit report to their publicly accessible websites or verifying that the audited entity has posted the audit report to its publicly accessible website.

Reporting Confidential or Sensitive Information

Requirements: Reporting Confidential or Sensitive Information

9.61 If certain information is prohibited from public disclosure or is excluded from a report because of its confidential or sensitive nature, auditors should disclose in the report that certain information has been omitted and the circumstances that make the omission necessary.

> **9.62** When circumstances call for omission of certain information, auditors should evaluate whether this omission could distort the audit results or conceal improper or illegal practices and revise the report language as necessary to avoid report users drawing inappropriate conclusions from the information presented.
>
> **9.63** When the audit organization is subject to public records laws, auditors should determine whether public records laws could affect the availability of classified or limited use reports and determine whether other means of communicating with management and those charged with governance would be more appropriate. Auditors use judgment to determine the appropriate means to communicate the omitted information to management and those charged with governance considering, among other things, whether public records laws could affect the availability of classified or limited use reports.

Application Guidance: Reporting Confidential or Sensitive Information

9.64 If the report refers to the omitted information, the reference may be general and not specific. If the omitted information is not necessary to meet the audit objectives, the report need not refer to its omission.

9.65 Certain information may be classified or may otherwise be prohibited from general disclosure by federal, state, or local laws or regulations. In such circumstances, auditors may issue a separate, classified, or limited use report containing such information and distribute the report only to persons authorized by law or regulation to receive it.

9.66 Additional circumstances associated with public safety, privacy, or security concerns could justify the exclusion of certain information from a publicly available or widely distributed report. For example, detailed information related to computer security for a particular program may be excluded from publicly available reports because of the potential damage that misuse of this information could cause. In such circumstances, auditors may issue a limited use report containing such information and distribute the report only to those parties responsible for acting on the auditors' recommendations. In some instances, it may be appropriate to issue both a publicly available report with the sensitive information excluded and a limited use report. The auditors may consult with legal counsel regarding any requirements or other circumstances that may necessitate omitting certain information. Considering the broad public interest in the program or activity under audit assists auditors when deciding whether to exclude certain information from publicly available reports.

9.67 In cases described in paragraph 9.63, auditors may communicate general information in a written report and communicate detailed information orally. Auditors may consult with legal counsel regarding applicable public records laws.

Discovery of Insufficient Evidence after Report Release

Requirement: Discovery of Insufficient Evidence after Report Release

9.68 If, after the report is issued, the auditors discover that they did not have sufficient, appropriate evidence to support the reported findings or conclusions, they should communicate in the same manner as that used to originally distribute the report to those charged with governance, the appropriate officials of the audited entity, the appropriate officials of the entities requiring or arranging for the audits, and other known users, so that they do not continue to rely on the findings or conclusions that were not supported. If the report was previously posted to the auditors' publicly accessible website, the auditors should remove the report and post a public notification that the report was removed. The auditors should then determine whether to perform the additional audit work necessary to either reissue the report, including any revised findings or conclusions, or repost the original report if the additional audit work does not result in a change in findings or conclusions.

Glossary

The following terms are provided to assist in clarifying the *Government Auditing Standards*. The most relevant paragraph numbers are provided for reference. When terminology differs from that used at an organization subject to generally accepted government auditing standards (GAGAS), auditors use professional judgment to determine if there is an equivalent term.

Abuse: Behavior that is deficient or improper when compared with behavior that a prudent person would consider reasonable and necessary business practice given the facts and circumstances, but excludes fraud and noncompliance with provisions of laws, regulations, contracts, and grant agreements. (paragraphs 6.23, 7.25, and 8.122)

Agreed-upon procedures engagement: Consists of auditors performing specific procedures on subject matter or an assertion and reporting findings without providing an opinion or a conclusion on it. (paragraph 1.18c)

Appropriateness: The measure of the quality of evidence that encompasses the relevance, validity, and reliability of evidence used for addressing the audit objectives and supporting findings and conclusions. (paragraph 8.102)

Attestation engagement: An examination, review, or agreed-upon procedures engagement conducted under the GAGAS attestation standards related to subject matter or an assertion that is the responsibility of another party. (paragraph 1.27a)

Audit: Either a financial audit or performance audit conducted in accordance with GAGAS. (paragraph 1.27b)

Audit objectives: What the audit is intended to accomplish. They identify the audit subject matter and performance aspects to be included. Audit objectives can be thought of as questions about the program that the auditors seek to answer based on evidence obtained and assessed against criteria. Audit objectives may also pertain to the current status or condition of a program. (paragraph 8.08)

Audit organization: A government audit entity or a public accounting firm or other audit entity that conducts GAGAS engagements. (paragraph 1.27c)

Glossary

Audit procedures: The specific steps and tests auditors perform to address the audit objectives. (paragraph 8.11)

Audit report: A report issued as a result of a financial audit, attestation engagement, review of financial statements, or performance audit conducted in accordance with GAGAS. (paragraph 1.27d)

Audit risk: The possibility that the auditors' findings, conclusions, recommendations, or assurance may be improper or incomplete. The assessment of audit risk involves both qualitative and quantitative considerations. (paragraph 8.16)

Audited entity: The entity that is subject to a GAGAS engagement, whether that engagement is a financial audit, attestation engagement, review of financial statements, or performance audit. (paragraph 1.27e)

Auditor: An individual assigned to planning, directing, performing engagement procedures or reporting on GAGAS engagements (including work on audits, attestation engagements, and reviews of financial statements) regardless of job title. Therefore, individuals who may have the title auditor, information technology auditor, analyst, practitioner, evaluator, inspector, or other similar titles are considered auditors under GAGAS. (paragraph 1.27f)

Bias threat: The threat that an auditor will, as a result of political, ideological, social, or other convictions, take a position that is not objective. (paragraph 3.30c)

Cause: The factor or factors responsible for the difference between the condition and the criteria, which may also serve as a basis for recommendations for corrective actions. (paragraphs 6.27, 7.29, and 8.126)

Competence: The knowledge, skills, and abilities, obtained from education and experience, necessary to conduct the GAGAS engagement. Competence enables auditors to make sound professional judgments. Competence includes possessing the technical knowledge and skills necessary for the assigned role and the type of work being done. This includes possessing specific knowledge about GAGAS. (paragraph 4.05)

Condition: A situation that exists. The condition is determined and documented during the engagement. (paragraphs 6.26, 7.28, and 8.125)

Glossary

Control objective: The aim or purpose of specified controls; control objectives address the risks related to achieving an entity's objectives. (paragraph 1.27g)

CPE programs: Structured educational activities or programs with learning objectives designed to maintain or enhance the auditors' competence to address engagement objectives and perform work in accordance with GAGAS. (paragraph 4.32)

Criteria: Laws, regulations, contracts, grant agreements, standards, measures, expected performance, defined business practices, and benchmarks against which performance is compared or evaluated. Criteria identify the required or desired state or expectation with respect to the program or operation. Criteria provide a context for evaluating evidence and understanding the findings, conclusions, and recommendations in the report. (paragraphs 6.25, 7.27, and 8.124)

Directing: Supervising the efforts of others who are involved in accomplishing the objectives of the engagement or reviewing engagement work to determine whether those objectives have been accomplished. (paragraph 4.11b)

Education: A structured and systematic process aimed at developing knowledge, skills, and other abilities; it is a process that is typically but not exclusively conducted in academic or learning environments. (paragraph 4.06)

Effect or potential effect: The outcome or consequence resulting from the difference between the condition and the criteria. (paragraphs 6.28, 7.30, and 8.127)

Engagement: A financial audit, attestation engagement, review of financial statements, or performance audit conducted in accordance with GAGAS. (paragraph 1.27h)

Engagement partner or director: The partner or director assigned responsibility for a specific engagement as designated by the audit organization. (paragraph 5.37)

Engagement team (or audit team): Auditors assigned to planning, directing, performing engagement procedures or reporting on GAGAS engagements. (paragraph 1.27i)

Glossary

Engaging party: The party that engages the auditor to conduct a GAGAS engagement. (paragraph 1.27j)

Entity objective: What an entity wants to achieve; entity objectives are intended to meet the entity's mission, strategic plan, and goals and the requirements of applicable laws and regulations. (paragraph 1.27k)

Examination: Consists of obtaining reasonable assurance by obtaining sufficient, appropriate evidence about the measurement or evaluation of subject matter against criteria in order to be able to draw reasonable conclusions on which to base the auditor's opinion about whether the subject matter is in accordance with (or based on) the criteria or the assertion is fairly stated, in all material respects. (paragraph 1.18a)

Experience: Workplace activities that are relevant to developing professional proficiency. (paragraph 4.06)

External audit organization: An audit organization that issues reports to third parties external to the audited entity, either exclusively or in addition to issuing reports to senior management and those charged with governance of the audited entity. (paragraph 1.27l)

Familiarity threat: The threat that aspects of a relationship with management or personnel of an audited entity, such as a close or long relationship, or that of an immediate or close family member, will lead an auditor to take a position that is not objective. (paragraph 3.30d)

Financial audits: Provide an independent assessment of whether an entity's reported financial information (e.g., financial condition, results, and use of resources) is presented fairly, in all material respects, in accordance with recognized criteria. (paragraph 1.17)

Finding: An issue that may involve a deficiency in internal control; noncompliance with provisions of laws, regulations, contracts, or grant agreements; or instances of fraud. Elements of a finding generally include criteria, condition, cause, and effect or potential effect. (paragraphs 6.17, 6.19, 7.19, 7.21, 8.116, and 8.118)

Fraud: Involves obtaining something of value through willful misrepresentation. Whether an act is, in fact, fraud is determined through the judicial or other adjudicative system and is beyond auditors' professional responsibility. (paragraph 8.73)

Independence in appearance: The absence of circumstances that would cause a reasonable and informed third party to reasonably conclude that the integrity, objectivity, or professional skepticism of an audit organization or member of the engagement team had been compromised. (paragraph 3.21b)

Independence of mind: The state of mind that permits the conduct of an engagement without being affected by influences that compromise professional judgment, thereby allowing an individual to act with integrity and exercise objectivity and professional skepticism. (paragraph 3.21a)

Inputs: The amount of resources (in terms of, for example, money, material, or personnel) that is put into a program. These resources may come from within or outside the entity operating the program. Measures of inputs can have a number of dimensions, such as cost, timing, and quality. (paragraph 8.38d)

Integrity: Auditors performing their work with an attitude that is objective, fact-based, nonpartisan, and nonideological with regard to audited entities and users of the audit reports and making decisions consistent with the public interest of the program or activity under audit. (paragraphs 3.09 and 3.10)

Internal audit organization: An audit organization that is accountable to senior management and those charged with governance of the audited entity and that does not generally issue reports to third parties external to the audited entity. (paragraph 1.27m)

Internal control: A process effected by an entity's oversight body, management, and other personnel that provides reasonable assurance that the objectives of an entity will be achieved. (paragraph 1.22b)

Likelihood of occurrence: The possibility of a deficiency impacting an entity's ability to achieve its objectives. (paragraph 8.56b)

Magnitude of impact: The likely effect that a deficiency could have on the entity achieving its objectives. (paragraph 8.56a)

Management participation threat: The threat that results from an auditor's taking on the role of management or otherwise performing management functions on behalf of the audited entity, which will lead an auditor to take a position that is not objective. (paragraph 3.30f)

Methodology: The nature and extent of audit procedures for gathering and analyzing evidence to address the audit objectives. (paragraph 8.11)

Monitoring of quality: A process comprising an ongoing consideration and evaluation of the audit organization's system of quality control. (paragraph 5.47)

Nature of the deficiency: Involves factors such as the degree of subjectivity involved with the deficiency and whether the deficiency arises from fraud or misconduct. (paragraph 8.56c)

Nonsupervisory auditor: An auditor who plans or performs engagement procedures and whose work situation is characterized by low levels of ambiguity, complexity, and uncertainty. (paragraph 4.10a)

Objectivity: The basis for the credibility of auditing in the government sector. Objectivity includes independence of mind and appearance when conducting engagements, maintaining an attitude of impartiality, having intellectual honesty, and being free of conflicts of interest. (paragraph 3.11)

Outcomes: Accomplishments or results of a program. (paragraph 8.38g)

Outputs: The quantity of goods or services produced by a program. (paragraph 8.38f)

Partners and directors: Auditors who plan engagements, perform engagement procedures, or direct or report on engagements and whose work situations are characterized by high levels of ambiguity, complexity, and uncertainty. Partners and directors may also be responsible for reviewing engagement quality prior to issuing the report, for signing the report, or both. (paragraph 4.10c)

Peer review risk: the risk that the review team (1) fails to identify significant weaknesses in the reviewed audit organization's system of quality control for its auditing practice, its lack of compliance with that system, or a combination thereof; (2) issues an inappropriate opinion on the reviewed audit organization's system of quality control for its auditing practice, its compliance with that system, or a combination thereof; or (3) makes an inappropriate decision about the matters to be included in, or excluded from, the peer review report. (paragraph 5.68)

Glossary

Performance audits: Engagements that provide objective analysis, findings, and conclusions to assist management and those charged with governance and oversight to, among other things, improve program performance and operations, reduce costs, facilitate decision making by parties with responsibility to oversee or initiate corrective action, and contribute to public accountability. In a performance audit, the auditors measure or evaluate the subject matter of the audit and present the resulting information as part of, or accompanying, the audit report. (paragraphs 1.21 and 8.14)

Period of professional engagement: The period beginning when the auditors either sign an initial engagement letter or other agreement to conduct an engagement or begin to conduct an engagement, whichever is earlier. The period lasts for the duration of the professional relationship—which, for recurring engagements, could cover many periods—and ends with the formal or informal notification, either by the auditors or the audited entity, of the termination of the professional relationship or with the issuance of a report, whichever is later. (paragraph 3.23)

Performing engagement procedures: Performing tests and procedures necessary to accomplish the engagement objectives in accordance with GAGAS. (paragraph 4.11c)

Planning: Determining engagement objectives, scope, and methodology; establishing criteria to evaluate matters subject to audit; or coordinating the work of the other audit organization. This definition excludes auditors whose role is limited to gathering information used in planning the engagement. (paragraph 4.11a)

Presumptively mandatory requirements: Auditors and the audit organization must comply in all cases where such a requirement is relevant except in rare circumstances discussed in paragraphs 2.03, 2.04, and 2.08. GAGAS uses *should* to indicate a presumptively mandatory requirement. (paragraph 2.02b)

Professional behavior: Behavior that includes auditors avoiding any conduct that could bring discredit to their work and putting forth an honest effort in performing their duties in accordance with the relevant technical and professional standards. (paragraph 3.16)

Professional judgment: Use of the auditor's professional knowledge, skills, and abilities, in good faith and with integrity, to diligently gather

Glossary

information and objectively evaluate the sufficiency and appropriateness of evidence. Professional judgment includes exercising reasonable care and professional skepticism. (paragraphs 3.109 through 3.117)

Program: Includes processes, projects, studies, policies, operations, activities, entities, and functions. (paragraph 8.08)

Program operations: The strategies, processes, and activities management uses to convert inputs into outputs. Program operations may be subject to internal control. (paragraph 8.38e)

Public interest: The collective well-being of the community of people and entities that the auditors serve. (paragraph 3.07)

Reasonable and informed third party: As evaluated by a hypothetical person, a person who possesses skills, knowledge, and experience to objectively evaluate the appropriateness of the auditor's judgments and conclusions. This evaluation entails weighing all the relevant facts and circumstances, including any safeguards applied, that the auditor knows, or could reasonably be expected to know, at the time that the evaluation is made. (paragraph 3.46)

Reporting: Determining the report content and substance or reviewing reports to determine whether the engagement objectives have been accomplished and the evidence supports the report's technical content and substance prior to issuance. This includes signing the report. (paragraph 4.11d)

Responsible party: The party responsible for a GAGAS engagement's subject matter. (paragraph 1.27n)

Review: Consists of obtaining limited assurance by obtaining sufficient, appropriate review evidence about the measurement or evaluation of subject matter against criteria in order to express a conclusion about whether any material modifications should be made to the subject matter in order for it to be in accordance with (or based on) the criteria or to the assertion in order for it to be fairly stated. Review-level work does not include reporting on internal control or compliance with provisions of laws, regulations, contracts, and grant agreements. (paragraph 1.18b)

Review of financial statements: The objective of the auditor when performing a review of financial statements is to obtain limited assurance as a basis for reporting whether the auditor is aware of any material modifications that should be made to financial statements in order for the financial statements to be in accordance with the applicable financial reporting framework. A review of financial statements does not include obtaining an understanding of the entity's internal control, assessing fraud risk, or certain other procedures ordinarily performed in an audit. (paragraph 1.20)

Safeguards: Actions or other measures, individually or in combination, that auditors and the audit organization take that effectively eliminate threats to independence or reduce them to an acceptable level. (paragraph 3.49)

Scope: The boundary of the audit and is directly tied to the audit objectives. The scope defines the subject matter that the auditors will assess and report on, such as a particular program or aspect of a program, the necessary documents or records, the period of time reviewed, and the locations that will be included. (paragraph 8.10)

Self-interest threat: The threat that a financial or other interest will inappropriately influence an auditor's judgment or behavior. (paragraph 3.30a)

Self-review threat: The threat that an auditor or audit organization that has provided nonaudit services will not appropriately evaluate the results of previous judgments made or services provided as part of the nonaudit services when forming a judgment significant to a GAGAS engagement. (paragraph 3.30b)

Significance: The relative importance of a matter within the context in which it is being considered, including quantitative and qualitative factors. In the performance audit requirements, the term significant is comparable to the term material as used in the context of financial statement engagements. (paragraph 8.15)

Source documents: Documents providing evidence that transactions have occurred (for example, purchase orders, payroll time records, customer orders, and contracts). Such records also include an audited entity's general ledger and subsidiary records or equivalent. (paragraph 3.92)

Specialist: An individual or organization possessing special skill or knowledge in a particular field other than accounting or auditing that

Glossary

assists auditors in conducting engagements. A specialist may be either an internal specialist or an external specialist. (paragraph 1.27p)

Structural threat: The threat that an audit organization's placement within a government entity, in combination with the structure of the government entity being audited, will affect the audit organization's ability to perform work and report results objectively. (paragraph 3.30g)

Sufficiency: A measure of the quantity of evidence used to support the findings and conclusions related to the audit objectives. (paragraph 8.99)

Supervisory auditor: An auditor who plans engagements, performs engagement procedures, or directs engagements, and whose work situation is characterized by moderate levels of ambiguity, complexity, and uncertainty. (paragraph 4.10b)

Technical comments: Comments that address points of fact or are editorial in nature and do not address substantive issues, such as methodology, findings, conclusions, or recommendations. (paragraphs 6.61, 7.59, and 9.54)

Those charged with governance: The individuals responsible for overseeing the strategic direction of the entity and obligations related to the accountability of the entity. This includes overseeing the financial reporting process, subject matter, or program under audit, including related internal controls. Those charged with governance may also be part of the entity's management. In some audited entities, multiple parties may be charged with governance, including oversight bodies, members or staff of legislative committees, boards of directors, audit committees, or parties contracting for the engagement. (paragraph 1.04)

Unconditional requirement: Requirement with which auditors and the audit organization must comply in all cases where such requirement is relevant. GAGAS uses *must* to indicate an unconditional requirement. (paragraph 2.02a)

Undue influence threat: The threat that influences or pressures from sources external to the audit organization will affect an auditor's ability to make objective judgments. (paragraph 3.30e)

Waste: The act of using or expending resources carelessly, extravagantly, or to no purpose. Waste can include activities that do not

Glossary

include abuse and does not necessarily involve a violation of law. (paragraphs 6.21, 7.23, and 8.120)

Acknowledgments

Comptroller General's Advisory Council on Government Auditing Standards (2016-2020)

Drummond Kahn, Chair
International Institute and Government Audit Training Institute
Graduate School USA

Corey Arvizu
Heinfeld, Meech & Co., P.C.

Dr. Brett M. Baker
U.S. Nuclear Regulatory Commission, Office of the Inspector General

Jon Hatfield
U.S. Federal Maritime Commission, Office of the Inspector General

Philip M. Heneghan
U.S. International Trade Commission, Office of the Inspector General

Mary L. Kendall
U.S. Department of the Interior, Office of the Inspector General

Deborah V. Loveless
Tennessee Comptroller of the Treasury, Division of State Audit

Martha S. Mavredes
Auditor of Public Accounts of the Commonwealth of Virginia

Kimberly K. McCormick
Grant Thornton LLP

Amanda Nelson
KPMG LLP

Dr. Demetra Smith Nightingale
Urban Institute

Dr. Annette K. Pridgen
Jackson State University

Dianne Ray
Colorado Office of the State Auditor

Harriet Richardson
City of Palo Alto

Randy C. Roberts
Arizona Office of the Auditor General

Brian A. Schebler
RSM US LLP

Ronald Smith
RHR Smith & Company CPAs

GAO Project Team

James R. Dalkin, Director
Kristen A. Kociolek, Assistant Director
Christie A. Pugnetti, Auditor in Charge
Michael F. Bingham, Senior Auditor
Mary Ann Hardy, Senior Auditor
Rebecca A. Riklin, Senior Auditor

J. Lawrence Malenich, Managing Director, Financial Management and Assurance
Robert F. Dacey, Chief Accountant

Staff Acknowledgments

In addition to the project team named above, also contributing were Mark Cheung, Clayton T. Clark, Oliver A. Culley, Francine M. DelVecchio, Vincent Gomes, John R. Grobarek, Sean P. Joyce, Jason M. Kelly, Delores J. Lee, Aaron M. Livernois, Quang D. Nguyen, Grant L. Simmons, Adrienne N. Walker, Kimberly Y. Young, and Matthew P. Zaun.

GAO's Mission	The Government Accountability Office, the audit, evaluation, and investigative arm of Congress, exists to support Congress in meeting its constitutional responsibilities and to help improve the performance and accountability of the federal government for the American people. GAO examines the use of public funds; evaluates federal programs and policies; and provides analyses, recommendations, and other assistance to help Congress make informed oversight, policy, and funding decisions. GAO's commitment to good government is reflected in its core values of accountability, integrity, and reliability.
Obtaining Copies of GAO Reports and Testimony	The fastest and easiest way to obtain copies of GAO documents at no cost is through GAO's website (https://www.gao.gov). Each weekday afternoon, GAO posts on its website newly released reports, testimony, and correspondence. To have GAO e-mail you a list of newly posted products, go to https://www.gao.gov and select "E-mail Updates."
Order Printed Copies	The printed version of the *Government Auditing Standards 2018 Revision* can be ordered through the Government Printing Office (GPO) online http://bookstore.gpo.gov/ or by calling 202-512-1800 or 1-866-512-1800 toll free.
Connect with GAO	Connect with GAO on Facebook, Flickr, Twitter, and YouTube. Subscribe to our RSS Feeds or E-mail Updates. Listen to our Podcasts. Visit GAO on the web at https://www.gao.gov.
To Report Fraud, Waste, and Abuse in Federal Programs	Contact: Website: https://www.gao.gov/fraudnet/fraudnet.htm Automated answering system: (800) 424-5454 or (202) 512-7470
Congressional Relations	Orice Williams Brown, Managing Director, WilliamsO@gao.gov, (202) 512-4400, U.S. Government Accountability Office, 441 G Street NW, Room 7125, Washington, DC 20548
Public Affairs	Chuck Young, Managing Director, youngc1@gao.gov, (202) 512-4800 U.S. Government Accountability Office, 441 G Street NW, Room 7149 Washington, DC 20548
Strategic Planning and External Liaison	James-Christian Blockwood, Managing Director, spel@gao.gov, (202) 512-4707 U.S. Government Accountability Office, 441 G Street NW, Room 7814, Washington, DC 20548

Please Print on Recycled Paper.

Made in the USA
Coppell, TX
16 May 2021